CR

J. Kerr

It's the
Final Score
That Counts

It's the Final Score That Counts

Edited by
Phyllis and Zander Hollander

An Associated Features Book

A THISTLE BOOK

Published by
GROSSET & DUNLAP, INC.
A National General Company
New York

To

Dr. Robert Blizzard
who helps the little guy to score

ACKNOWLEDGMENTS

We play the role of producers. When you have a cast of characters that ranges from Chuck Connors, Brud Holland and Whizzer White to Bob Mathias, Bob Pettit and Benjamin Spock, you need a matching set of writers. We are grateful to Ira Berkow of Newspaper Enterprise Association, Larry Fox of the New York *Daily News,* Joe Gergen of *Newsday,* Sandy Padwe of *Newsday,* Marty Ralbovsky of *The New York Times,* and George Solomon of the Washington *Post* for their contributions. And we thank the players for their cooperation.

A special note of appreciation to Ben Mintz of Cornell University, Les Unger of Rutgers, Al Shrier of Temple, Clary Anderson and Butch Fortunato of Montclair, New Jersey, and the many friends of Buzz Aldrin.

Phyllis and Zander Hollander
Baldwin, New York

Photo Credits

The editors and publisher wish to thank the following individuals and organizations for their courtesy in making their photos available for this book:

NASA: Facing page I (also cover).

Richard Brown: Page 5.

Newark *News*: Page 5 (bottom).

Bob Mathias: Page 10.

Chuck Connors: Cover, pages 20, 23.

Suzanne Szasz: Page 32.

Alfred Hedén: Page 42.

Cornell University: Page 45.

Dr. Jerome Holland: Page 48.

ABC-TV: Page 52.

J. Consentino: Page 72.

Temple University: Page 86.

CBS-TV: Page 82.

Dr. Benjamin Spock: Page 100.

United Press International, Inc.: Pages 16 (also cover), 36 (also cover), 55, 68, 89, 93, 96, 104, 110, 112.

Bob Pettit: Page 62.

New York Yankees: Page 59 (also cover).

CONTENTS

INTRODUCTION

Ever since boy—or girl—has been given his first football, bat, basketball, skates or whatever piece of sporting equipment, it has been the ticket to fun, games and dreams. Indeed, to the youngster growing up on the playing fields the ultimate in achievement is often represented by the superstars of sport with all the glamor, money and fame.

When Buzz Aldrin was a schoolboy he pictured himself as one day being a football player at Notre Dame. Bill Cosby wanted to be a pro halfback, Tenley Albright an Olympic figure skating champion, Jim Bouton a major league baseball player.

As with the other notables in the starting lineup of IT'S THE FINAL SCORE THAT COUNTS, all had a common love of sport and a desire to succeed in their respective specialties.

They pitched, ran, pole-vaulted, rowed and tackled for school, for country or just for themselves. As athletes, whether on amateur or professional levels, they ascended to various plateaus of excellence. But their playing days were to serve as something more than the stuff that scrapbooks and dreams are made of.

With sport as a training ground, a launching platform, they left the arena to contribute to the greater world outside. One landed on the moon, another became a surgeon . . . a sports announcer . . . an actor . . . an ambassador . . . an advertising executive . . . a comedian . . . a chairman of the board of a bank . . . a Supreme Court Justice . . . a Congressman . . . a candidate for the Presidency of the United States.

The discipline, competitiveness, teamwork and inspiration that came out of athletics had helped each one achieve goals beyond the stadium.

It's the
Final Score
That Counts

Buzz Aldrin, ex-pole vaulter, takes a walk on the moon.

BUZZ ALDRIN
VAULTING TO THE MOON

THE PRESIDENT OF the United States was on the telephone. It was a long distance call from Washington, D.C. to the Sea of Tranquility on the moon—250,000 miles.

PRESIDENT NIXON: "Hello, Neil and Buzz, I am talking to you from the Oval Room at the White House. And this certainly has to be the most historic telephone call ever made. I just can't tell you how proud we all are of you . . . and for people all over the world, I am sure that they too join with Americans in recognizing what an immense feat this is. Because of what you have done, the heavens have become a part of man's world . . ."

NEIL ARMSTRONG: "Thank you, Mr. President. It's a great honor and privilege for us to be here representing not only the United States but men of peace of all nations . . . men with a vision for the future."

THE PRESIDENT: "I look forward to seeing you on the *Hornet* next Thursday."

ARMSTRONG: "Thank you."

BUZZ ALDRIN: "I look forward to that very much, sir."

The day was July 20, 1969. Minutes before, Colonel Edwin E. (Buzz) Aldrin Jr. had exclaimed, "Beautiful, beautiful," as he stepped on the moon's surface, the second

1

man in history to do so. The first had been Neil Armstrong, who preceded Buzz by 19 minutes.

In Glen Ellyn, Illinois, Richard Brown, a boyhood friend of Aldrin's, wasn't surprised at Buzz's achievement. "Why, I remember the time Buzz swam 400 yards underwater," he said with a chuckle. "At least there were many who thought he did."

Whether underwater or literally, "out of this world," Buzz Aldrin early in life had shown signs of being one who knew where he was going and how to get there. Even to the moon.

Buzz was born in Montclair, New Jersey, in 1930. Oddly enough, his maternal grandfather's name was Moon—F. Arnold Moon, a chaplain in the United States Coast Guard. And his father was a pilot and a student of Dr. Robert Goddard, who was known as "The Father of Rocketry." The senior Aldrin was a friend of Orville Wright, who with his brother Wilbur built and flew the first successful airplane. Mr. Aldrin also knew Charles (Slim) Lindbergh, the first man to fly across the Atlantic Ocean alone.

Buzz's dad, who was to become a colonel in the United States Air Force during World War II, was active in commercial aviation, and he flew in various exhibitions in the U.S. and Europe. In the year Buzz was born, his dad flew a single-engine Lockheed Vega over the Alps in Europe. Three years later, Buzz had his first plane ride when Mr. Aldrin flew him to Miami, a ten-and-a-half-hour ride during which Buzz became airsick.

By the time he was nine, Buzz had been to a number of air shows with his father, and in 1939 he'd tried the parachute jump at the New York World's Fair in Flushing, New York. Buzz wasn't *that* impressed because the jump was not a free fall; it was controlled.

The Aldrins lived in a big house on Princeton Place in Montclair, across the street from the Ferguson family. Harold Ferguson had been a fraternity brother of the senior Aldrin at Clark University, and his son Dick was friendly with Buzz and his two older sisters, Fay and Madeline.

It was young Ferguson who built a rope swing on a big oak in the Aldrin backyard, where Buzz first showed an interest in gymnastics. Buzz, whose nickname was the result of sister Fay's garbled pronunciation of "Baby Brother," was a natural athlete. When he entered kindergarten at Edgemont Elementary School he was discovered to be unusually alert, happy at the science table and full of energy and enterprise in the games that youngsters play.

"He was quick and decisive, and he liked adventure," said Albert Hartman, his Edgemont principal. "Even in games like dodge ball, he would show ingenuity. If they were choosing up sides for something, he would always be the first chosen—not because he was the biggest, he wasn't, but because everybody knew he would get there first."

In the summer when he was nine Buzz discovered a new world at the Trout Lake Camp in East Stoneham, Maine. He went there for seven summers, as camper and in the end as counselor-in-training. There Buzz was Mr. All-Around Camper. Dick Ferguson, his friend from Montclair, was a counselor at Trout Lake and a track man. He was largely responsible for the building of a combination high-jumping, pole-vaulting and broad-jumping pit of sawdust, sand and clay at the camp. Buzz developed a keen interest in pole-vaulting. He was also one of the fastest swimmers in camp.

Everyone looked up to Buzz. One day, Charles Hamilton, director of the camp, decided to give the youngsters a demonstration of Aldrin's talents in the water. "We sat the entire camp on shore, and Buzz went out to a float about fifty feet offshore," Hamilton said. "We told the kids that Buzz would swim down the lake underwater and suggested they keep an eye on the counselors in the rowboat which would follow him."

Buzz dived off the float and disappeared. The counselors rowed off, presumably on Buzz's course. From time to time they would stand up and cheer, and the campers would cheer too, although they found it hard to believe that Buzz could stay under that long. Finally, some 400 yards from the float, a figure rose from the water and the campers roared their approval. Then, almost in a chorus, they shouted, "Let him swim back the same way."

Eventually, back at the float where it had all begun, Buzz emerged, out of breath but triumphant. "It's impossible," some of the older boys insisted. But Mr. Hamilton, who had offered five dollars to Buzz if he made good, publicly paid him off on the beach, and everyone seemed to be convinced that this was an authentic swim. As one camper said, "He must have done it; Mr. Hamilton wouldn't part with anything if he didn't have to."

Of course, it was a gag. Buzz had stayed out of sight behind the float, and somebody else with the same towhead and build had come out of the water 400 yards away.

Dick Brown, one of Buzz's fellow campers, also remembered a day when Mr. Aldrin came to Trout Lake and they got to talking about the speed of airplanes. This was in 1939 and Buzz's flying father predicted, "One day you'll see planes flying at better than 500 miles an hour."

Back in Montclair, Buzz had moved up from Edgemont to Mt. Hebron Junior High and then to Montclair High. All the time, he was building himself up physically. A friend, Russell Long, helped Buzz erect a high bar for gymnastics in the Aldrin backyard. Showing endurance and skill, Buzz did handsprings and backflips, he worked on the rings and horses, and did pushups, situps and pullups. Whenever they gave tests at school he was at or near the top.

Mentally he proved to be a whiz too—in and out of the classroom. Buzz loved to work on problems of logic; he had tremendous ability to concentrate and was a model of self-discipline. He worked on odd, self-inspired projects. One such project involved development of a system for beating the roulette wheel. In the Aldrin basement on a Ping-pong table he also made a layout of squares and developed his own soldier-strategy game. "We called him Mrs. Aldrin's All-American boy," Russell Long said. "And we did so with the fullest respect."

Sports always were a big part of Buzz's life; by the time he entered high school he was eager about football and pole-vaulting. He had dreamed of playing football for Notre Dame, but as a sophomore halfback in 1944 he didn't get a minute of playing time on Coach Angelo (Butch) Fortunato's varsity team.

Buzz did, however, show promise as a pole-vaulter. He tied for first in the Montclair Invitation Meet and tied again with his teammate, Alan Heil, in the state championships. His best height as a sophomore was 10-6, with a bamboo pole.

Buzz didn't try out for football in 1945. He'd made up his mind that he wanted to better his grades in order to improve

Camper Aldrin (back row, left) at Trout Lake in Maine.

Buzz Aldrin centers Montclair High's championship team.

his chances for admission to the United States Military Academy.

He did find time to work at George Bond's ice cream parlor, which featured a milkshake called an Awful Awful. It had four scoops of ice cream, and anybody who could drink three of them would get a fourth at no cost. But the fourth had to be taken outside. The proprietor did not want to risk his young patrons' becoming ill inside the shop. A few lived through four Awful Awfuls.

At school, Buzz's grades as he became an upperclassman were mostly A's. One of his math teachers, Bill Filas, said: "He seemed to enjoy success where you can see success, as in solving math problems. There was no attempt to outshine other students on a commonplace problem, but when it came to deep analysis and thought, he had his drive to excel. He was a natural in mathematics, and he gave the appearance of being absolutely sure of himself at all times."

When Buzz reported for his senior year in September of 1947, he decided to try out for football again. Clary Anderson, returned from the war, was back as head coach and he was loaded with backfield candidates, including a 5-foot-9, 165-pounder called Buzz Aldrin. But Anderson didn't have a center.

"Son," he said, singling out Buzz, "I'd like to give you a chance in the backfield, but we've got so many veterans I doubt you'll be any higher than third-string. The quickest way to the first team is to play center. How would you like to try it?"

"Show me what I have to do," Buzz replied in an instant, and he became an instant center.

He learned how to snap the ball between his legs and then fire out at the defense. At a time when few centers did so, Buzz used one hand for centering the ball, even on punts. He felt more comfortable with one hand and he could take off much better.

"This was innovative on his part," Anderson pointed out. "And he never made a bad pass."

The Montclair team proceeded to win every game that season, and that brought Buzz and his mates the state championship. Buzz had not only proved himself as an offensive player but he'd stood out as a pass defender and an astute reader of the opposition's plays.

It was quite a senior year for Buzz. In track he repeatedly topped 11 feet in the pole vault. He tied for first in the Newark Invitation and was second in the state championships. His best height was 11-6. To cap it all, he was awarded the Woodman Track Trophy for "excellence in track accomplishments, leadership and scholastic pursuits."

In addition, Buzz's essay, "Plans and Compromises of the Constitution," won the contest conducted by the Sons of the American Revolution. Fittingly, Buzz had begun his essay with a sports analogy: There were two boys from the same baseball team, each wanting to pitch. Buzz settled things by having each pitch half a game, "a compromise which is the basis of all great documents," he wrote.

Essayist Aldrin's conclusion: "These 55 men at Philadelphia (who wrote the Constitution) displayed their greatness to such an extent . . . that many of our present-day statesmen would do well to follow their example of the true American spirit: to cooperate with, rather than fight, those of divergent viewpoints. When two opposing factions meet, there is only one just and equal solution—a compromise."

Buzz's many accomplishments did not go unnoticed. One day there was a call from Senator Albert W. Hawkes. "Young man, I'm pleased to be able to say that you have an appointment to the United States Military Academy," he told a jubilant Buzz.

The senior class labeled Mrs. Aldrin's All-American boy as the one "most likely to succeed," and the yearbook forecast that he would "become a general in the lower Slovovian Army."

That summer of 1947 Buzz was seventeen when he went off to West Point, New York, home of the U.S. Military Academy. He was too small for varsity football, but he did play some intramural ball. And he decided to concentrate on his pole-vaulting—that is, when he wasn't studying. At the end of his first year, Buzz was No. 1 in his class.

By the time Carl Crowell came to West Point as track and field coach, Buzz was a senior. "I was impressed with how Buzz took his practice so seriously," Crowell said. "He was a perfectionist in pole-vaulting as he was in everything else. He practiced in the usual way, but he tried harder. He ran, he lifted weights, worked on the parallel bars and the horizontal bars, climbed ropes and jumped.''

Buzz soared to a top height of 13-8, ⅛ shy of the West Point Field House record. He finished in second-place ties in the IC4A championships and in the Heptagonals. The 13-8 figure was very respectable; fiberglass poles, like trips to the moon, were not yet fashionable.

He graduated No. 3 in his class in 1951 and moved on to Bryan Field, Texas, where he won his Air Force wings. Before going to Korea, Buzz married Joan Archer. In Korea he flew 66 missions, destroying two MIGs and damaging others. He won the Distinguished Flying Cross, among other decorations.

After Korea came a tour of duty in West Germany, but Buzz was not satisfied with simply being an Air Force pilot. As he had throughout his life, Buzz sought new challenges, and the Air Force sent him to Massachusetts Institute of Technology for advanced schooling. In 1963, he wrote his dissertation on orbital mechanics and dedicated it to "the men in the astronaut program." In his conclusion, Buzz wrote, "Oh, that I was one of them!"

Indeed, he wanted more than anything to get into the space project. In many ways he'd been preparing for it since the days when he built and flew model airplanes out of the third-floor window in the big house in Montclair.

The National Aeronautics and Space Administration (NASA) set rigid requirements for its astronauts, one of which was that you had to be a test pilot. Buzz was not a test pilot. But in 1963, NASA dropped this requirement and let in combat pilots with 1,000 hours of jet experience. Buzz was accepted as an astronaut.

Three years later, in November of 1966, Buzz was finally up in space—on the Gemini 12 spacecraft as it whirled around on a four-day flight. This included dockings with an Agena rocket and open-hatch maneuvers in which Buzz leaned halfway out of the spacecraft to take pictures and do exercises. Even more dramatic was his leaving the capsule completely for five-and-a-half hours, attached to a 25-foot tether as he exposed himself to the raw environment.

Buzz returned to his home town of Montclair the following

month and at Woodman Field, where he had excelled as an athlete, the astronaut told the audience, mostly young people: "All individuals should reach for excellence in whatever they do. But be realistic. Not everyone can be above average. Each person can be excellent in one particular way."

Now Buzz was reaching for the moon. Three very special men had been chosen for the mission that would rank them with history's most illustrious and daring explorers. And Buzz was one of them, along with Neil Armstrong and Mike Collins.

They would all start out together on the space aircraft *Columbia*, then Armstrong and Aldrin would take off in the lunar module *Eagle* that would separate from the mother ship and make a landing on the surface of the moon. Nobody had ever been on the moon.

At 9:32 A.M. on July 16, 1969, as orange flames and dark smoke poured out of the Saturn 5 rocket supporting it, the 3,817-ton Apollo spacecraft blasted off from Cape Kennedy.

In Washington, D.C., Vince Lombardi of the Washington Redskins football team stopped practice and asked his players to pray for the three astronauts. "This is something transcending what we all do," he said. "I'm conscious that there are a hell of a lot of things more important than football—and you know how much I like football—and this is one."

The whole world was watching and rooting. And they would not be disappointed. Four days after launch, the word from *Eagle* was: "Houston, Tranquility Base here. The *Eagle* has landed."

Six-and-a-half hours later, Neil Armstrong became the first man to set foot on the moon. He was followed by Buzz Aldrin. They went about a series of tasks, planting an American flag, gathering moon rocks and setting seismic experiments.

The next day, the astronauts blasted the lunar module off the moon and rejoined *Columbia*. They jettisoned *Eagle* and then began the return flight to earth. "It's nice to sit here and watch the earth getting larger and larger and the moon smaller and smaller," Aldrin said.

On July 24—eight days, three hours and 18 minutes from launch—*Columbia* splashed down in the Pacific Ocean.

The ex-pole vaulter and his companions had taken a giant leap for mankind.

Congressman Mathias represents California's 18th District.

BOB MATHIAS
OLYMPIAN IN WASHINGTON

ON THE MORNING of August 5, 1948, Bob Mathias, a seventeen-year-old boy, rode on a bus with members of the U.S. track and field team to Wembley Stadium in the London suburbs. Though young enough to be the waterboy, Mathias was about to compete for the most grueling prize in sports—the Olympic decathlon championship.

Mathias curled his 6-foot-2, 190-pound frame into one of the seats, ignoring the drizzling rain. He was either very much worried or else unusually impassive about the whole thing.

A teammate, knowing Mathias was the youngest member of the track and field squad, said, "Don't worry, Bob, you'll be all right."

Mathias raised his head and smiled. "I'm okay," he said. "You don't get any points for worrying."

Five months earlier, Robert Bruce Mathias was unknown outside of California's San Joaquin Valley, where he was an all-sports star at Tulare High School. In March of 1948, he didn't even know the ten events of the decathlon, much less possess any ambitions of becoming a gold medal winner.

Tulare's coach, Virgil Jackson, was so impressed with

11

Mathias' showings in the hurdles, discus and high jump that he urged his prize pupil to attempt the decathlon, thinking four years ahead hopefully to the 1952 Olympics. Jackson secured several coaching manuals, Mathias began working and things happened. Bob, though he had never before thrown a javelin or shot-put, or run 400 meters and 1,500 meters in competition, stunned the sports world with unexpected victories in the Southern Pacific Amateur Athletic Union Games and Olympic trials. He had made the Olympic Team four years ahead of schedule.

"It's happening too fast for me to realize what's going on," Mathias said. "I'm scared to death by the whole business."

But now all this was behind him, and the Olympics had begun.

The first three decathlon events—100-meter dash, broad jump and shot-put—did not go well for Bob. Enrique Kistenmacher, an Argentine army officer, and Ignace Heinrich, a Frenchman, were solidly in command. A mediocre performance in the high jump would have finished the eager teenager from California. Twice he failed at 5 feet 9 inches. He had one more chance.

In the rain and gloom, Bob Mathias wrapped himself in a blanket and thought, *Forget about form. Just get over the bar.* Instead of approaching from the side of the crossbar as he normally did, Mathias frantically charged almost directly in front of it, and leaped awkwardly over the barrier.

Brutus Hamilton, the veteran track coach at the University of California, watching the drama from the stands, turned to a friend and shouted, "The kid's going to win it!"

Bob went on to clear 6-1¼, and after the first day's competition was 49 points behind Kistenmacher; 32 behind Heinrich. Before the next day's events began, Kistenmacher informed his younger rival, "Mathematically, I have it figured out you can't beat me." Mathias didn't say anything. He simply cleared 11-5¾ to win the pole vault; captured the javelin; and at 11 P.M., with the rain pelting down on the track, rumbled home first in the 1,500-meter to become the youngest decathlon champion in Olympic history.

In the stands, his brothers, Gene and Jimmy, cheered loudly. His parents, Dr. and Mrs. Charles Mathias, could only look at each other in amazement. Their son had accomplished the impossible.

When it was over, Bob Mathias said, "I never worked so long and so hard for anything in my life. I wouldn't do this again for a million dollars."

"We sent a boy over to do a man's job and he did it far better than any man ever could," said Paul Helms, the founder of the Helms Athletic Foundation.

"My life changed," Bob said. "In four months I went from being another high school senior to an Olympic champion. It was a hectic four months."

While nobody had predicted an Olympic gold medal for Bob, there was much in his formative years in Tulare that shaped him for it. The old family house was within two blocks of two school playgrounds and a gymnasium, which meant the three Mathias boys were always either running around a track or catching and shooting some kind of ball. The signal for mealtime was Mrs. Mathias blowing her whistle, easily audible from two blocks away.

At eleven, Bob Mathias already was high-jumping five feet and broad-jumping 15 feet. Incredibly, that same year, the future decathlon champion suffered from anemia, a quantitative deficiency of the red blood corpuscles, resulting in a general overall weakness to the system. Forced by his father, a general practitioner of medicine, to rest more frequently, Mathias did not allow the condition to hamper his progression in sports. He built up his body and had overcome his ailment by the time he entered high school.

At Tulare High, Mathias was to become a living legend in California sports. He set records in the hurdles, high-jump and discus; he was a brilliant tailback and a skillful center on the basketball team.

"Give up football and basketball," a well-meaning college track coach advised Mathias before his senior season. At the age of seventeen, Bob Mathias wasn't thinking about victory ceremonies or decathlons. He was a gifted athlete with a normal personality just looking to help his high school football and basketball teams win games.

Mathias' coach at Tulare, Virgil Jackson, had no experience with the decathlon. He was aware that there are ten events—100-meter dash, broad jump, shot-put, high jump,

400-meter run, 110-meter hurdles, discus, pole vault, javelin and 1,500-meter run. The first five events are run the first day; the second five the next. The key requirements for the event are overall athletic skill, physical stamina and love of competition. Jackson knew Bob was a fierce competitor who could develop the skills necessary to master the decathlon. The stamina factor remained a question mark, up until the time Mathias crossed the finish line in the 1,500-meter run, that rainy night at Wembley Stadium.

"Virgil Jackson got me interested and excited about the decathlon," Mathias said. "He changed my life. I had never even heard of the decathlon until he brought it up."

Bob Mathias had a rare gift of being able to isolate himself from conditions surrounding an event. He could attack a problem or goal with total concentration, blotting out of his mind everything except the immediate problem of competition. Some called him blase. Others, more knowledgeable, knew it was Mathias' way of preparing himself for the impending confrontation.

When he returned from the 1948 Olympics he played football and ran track at Kiski Prep School in Saltsburg, Pennsylvania, and later at Stanford University. He seemed oblivious to the pressures of being a national hero. He was just trying to be a student. In his first two years at Stanford, he did not go out for the football team, to the dismay of Stanford's alumni. He wanted to concentrate on his studies, hoping some day to enter medical school. By his junior year, he had abandoned that plan, realistically admitting he didn't have the aptitude for a medical career. Mathias never kidded anyone, including himself.

He turned out for the football team in the fall of 1951, and while the skeptics snickered when he fractured a toe in an early scrimmage, Mathias dogmatically kept plugging away. He rode the bench much of the early season as Stanford, a surprise in the Pacific Coast Conference, was beating everyone. When the two fullbacks ahead of Mathias were hurt, he got his chance.

"I play football for the same reason I run track," Mathias said. "I love to compete. Just being on the field, trying your hardest, that's what it's all about. If you win, you're all the more happy. Professional football never enters my mind. I play football as a hobby. That's why I enjoy it so much."

When Mathias returned a kickoff 96 yards for a touchdown to help Stanford beat Southern California and gain a spot in the Rose Bowl, he could have run for Governor of California and won easily.

Mathias worked long and hard for the 1952 Olympic Games, which were in Helsinki, Finland. If successful, he would become the first athlete ever to win the Olympic decathlon twice. Despite a painful injury to his thigh, he was magnificent, winning the gold medal with a record 7,887 points. In the two events which always gave Bob the most difficulty—the pole vault and 1,500-meter run—he was sensational.

Because of his size—he was tall and husky—Mathias had difficulty mastering the pole vault. Yet he managed to clear 13-6$\frac{1}{16}$ for 745 points. In the 1,500 meters, the final event of the two-day ordeal, he recorded a 4:50.8.

His victory was greeted with enthusiasm by the people of Finland. Bob Mathias had become something of a U.S. goodwill ambassador, easily making friends among athletes of all nations, including the Russians, who in 1952 had few friends among Westerners. Mathias was the epitome of the Olympic spirit.

"The idea of the Olympic Games is to foster international good will and sportsmanship," he said. "I truly believe in this, and did my best to generate whatever good will I could.

"The Olympic Village is like a 70-ring circus when all the athletes gather around to look at each other. They slap backs and swap souvenirs. You'd have to be a hard-nosed hermit to resist the spirit of good will."

He helped two Russian discus throwers by letting them use his resin. That was Mathias' way. He also beat both Russians in the discus throw, which says something else about him.

He will never forget his two victory ceremonies. "You're facing the flagstaff and the band strikes up the National Anthem. They run the flag of the United States to the top of the pole, and thousands of your countrymen explode with a sound that shakes the stadium. If anyone has the words to tell what you feel like then, it isn't me. It's a poet."

Bob Mathias hurls discus on the way to Olympic gold medal.

Mathias retired from active athletic competition following his Olympic triumph in 1952. He served two years as an officer in the Marine Corps, then became a representative for the Amateur Athletic Union and the U.S. State Department. On five occasions, Mathias was dispatched by the State Department to Europe, Asia, Africa and Latin America to organize and encourage sports and youth programs in various countries. He was President Eisenhower's personal representative to the 1956 Olympic Games in Melbourne, Australia. Mathias then tried his hand at public relations and television work, and even did a brief stint as a movie actor when he played himself in *The Bob Mathias Story.*

Bob first began thinking about politics on his initial European tour. The athletes would all gather after meals to talk, and the conversation usually reverted to politics and world events.

It was not unnatural that the former boy wonder from Tulare would consider a career in government. In November of 1966, he ran for Congress on the Democratic ticket and was elected as a Representative in California's 18th Congressional District. He was re-elected in 1968 and 1970, and again in 1972.

In the corridor of the Longworth Building adjacent to the U.S. Capitol, Mathias walks briskly from his office to the chambers of the U.S. House of Representatives. There is no mistaking his broad shoulders and assured gait. Even in the hallowed halls of Congress, Bob looks like an athlete.

When he walks into the House, there are no cheers. In an Olympics, the man who runs the fastest and jumps the highest achieves the honors. In the Congress of the United States, much of the running is done behind closed doors in smoke-filled committee rooms and on the telephone.

As Mathias sits behind the large mahogany desk working on papers and answering the phone, Wembley Stadium in London seems, and is, long ago. What matters now are his constituents in the California counties of Amador, Calaveras, Inyo, Madera, Mono, Mariposa, Tulare and Tuolumne, as well as portions of Kern, Merced and Stanislaus.

Always a man of speed and action, he quickly discovered upon arriving in Washington it takes longer to master the complexities of the federal government than the ten events of the decathlon.

"Accomplishing things in Washington takes time," he said. "A lot of freshmen congressmen try to set the world on fire their first year. They aren't successful. You don't make your contacts and find out who can help overnight."

Apart from his efforts involving matters in his own district, Mathias has been active in support of ecology legislation. In the 92nd Congress, he introduced the California Desert Bill, designed to protect ecological, economic and recreational resources, all of which he says are in danger of being destroyed in the California desert's twelve million acres of public lands.

During the legislative sessions, Mathias, his wife Melba and their three daughters live in Falls Church, Virginia. Once the greatest athlete in the world, he occasionally plays paddleball in the House of Representatives gymnasium. When he finds the time, he gets to ski on a weekend.

He remains involved in amateur athletics, helping the U.S. Olympic Committee in fund-raising projects and representing various amateur sports organizations. He also runs the Bob Mathias Boys and Girls Camps, located in the Sierra Nevada mountains. He enjoys being with young people.

"After my first Olympic decathlon I told some people I wouldn't do that again for a million dollars," Mathias said. "I didn't really mean that. When you've completed a decathlon, you're so exhausted it's impossible to explain. Later, when you've recovered some of your energy, you realize what you've done and the friendships you've acquired. That's when you know it's all worth it."

As a Congressman, Mathias views his role as "fascinating and a great challenge. It's the most interesting thing I've ever done. When I stop feeling this way, I'll find something else to do."

CHUCK CONNORS
ALWAYS IN THE ACT

WILLIE MAYS, a rookie with the New York Giants but already tabbed for future greatness, drew a walk his first time at bat against the Cubs one sunny afternoon in Chicago during the summer of 1951. As was his habit, he quickly struck up a conversation with Chicago's first baseman.

"Hey, aren't you Chuck Connors?" Willie asked in his high-pitched voice. "Boy, I've heard all about you. You really can recite. How about giving me some of that 'Casey at the Bat?' "

Flattered that the rookie was aware of his fame as a speaker and reciter of poetry, and already with a bit of the ham bursting out from beneath his baseball cap, Chuck Connors could not resist.

Striking a dramatic stance, he began, "The outlook wasn't brilliant for the Mudville nine . . ." when suddenly he was aware that he had lost his audience. There was a cackling from the area of second base. Willie Mays hadn't stuck around for the full performance. While Connors was reciting, Willie had stolen second.

In 1951, Kevin (Chuck) Connors was still a fulltime ball player and amateur performer. Soon, for the man who would

19

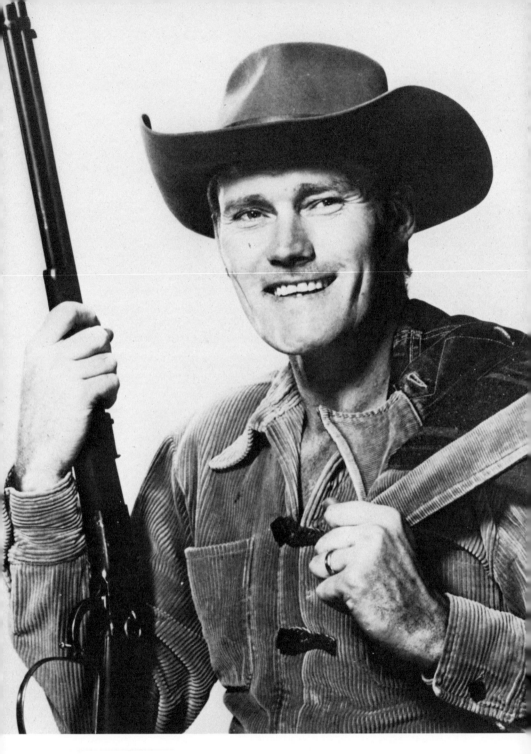

Chuck's most famous television role was as "The Rifleman."

win fame as television's Rifleman, these roles would be reversed. But in the beginning, it was all sports.

Chuck was born in 1921 in the Bay Ridge section of Brooklyn. Before he was ten years old, the Great Depression had laid its hand upon the nation, bringing poverty and unemployment. Bay Ridge did not escape. Chuck's father lost his job and would be out of work for years. His mother went to work as a scrubwoman. When food was scarce, Chuck would eat dinner at his aunt's house.

Trouble and more poverty awaited the children of Bay Ridge, but one man dedicated himself to helping the boys of his neighborhood escape this trap. His name was John Flynn, and he was a bank executive. A natty dresser who stood only 5-foot-5, Flynn had no children of his own so he adopted the boys of the neighborhood by forming a club called the Bay Ridge Celtics.

The Celtics fielded teams in all the sports, and Flynn would write instructional letters on how to play the various positions in different games. But, more important, he set up the club on a fully organized basis. There were weekly meetings in one boy's apartment or another and regular events scheduled to raise money. Connors served as secretary for five years. "The thing Mr. Flynn did was give us ideas about how we could raise money and then he left it up to us to carry them out. It gave us a sense of responsibility," Chuck said.

The boys staged dances and raffles and some weekends took off in teams of two or three with buckets and mops to scrub kitchens for neighborhood housewives. They'd charge a quarter or 50 cents for the chore. One day the Brooklyn *Eagle,* a newspaper, pointed out that the Bay Ridge Celtics' uniforms, costing $36.50 apiece, actually were more expensive than those of the Brooklyn Dodgers. The boys were really proud, and Chuck's mother saw to it that all the boys' uniforms were clean and mended.

Flynn, whom Connors calls "the biggest influence in my life," helped the boys in another important way. He stressed the value of schooling. After Connors' first year at Manual Training High, he arranged for Chuck to receive a scholarship at Brooklyn's Adelphi Academy. (Later Flynn also got Chuck's father a job.)

Connors blossomed at Adelphi under the tutoring of coach Hollis (Babe) Spotts. He starred in baseball, basketball and football, participated in track, wrote a gossip column in the school paper, was paid ten cents an inch space rates as correspondent for the Brooklyn *Eagle* and earned local fame for his recitations. He even had cards printed pointing out that he was available to perform at weddings and Bar Mitzvahs.

During this time, he grew to his full height of 6-5½, won all-star recognition in football and was tabbed "a big league prospect" at first base by Lou Miller of the New York *World-Telegram*.

Chuck also continued to play baseball for the Bay Ridge Celtics. Games were played in the Parade Grounds, a Brooklyn landmark consisting of a dozen diamonds, where two members of the team would be dispatched on Saturday nights with blankets to sleep over so they would be first on line to reserve the best field Sunday morning. Chuck's mother usually would arrive late for these games, and play would be halted as she marched across the diamond from the bus stop and took her seat in the grandstand.

When Chuck graduated from Adelphi Academy, he went downtown to the offices of the Brooklyn *Eagle* to settle up his correspondent's account with sports editor Lou Niss.

"Well, now that you've finished school, what are you going to do, Kevin?" Niss asked.

"I'd like to play professional baseball," the lad replied. Niss said, "Let me see if I can't make a phone call for you."

Diagonally across the street from the *Eagle* were the offices of the Brooklyn Dodgers, and Niss made his call to Branch Rickey, Jr., who headed the scouting department.

"I've never seen this kid play," Niss told young Rickey, "but I know he's over 6-5 and he batted .480 for four years as a left-handed hitting first baseman. He played on the football team, so that means he has strength; he played on the basketball team, so that means he has good hands; and he is the Academy quarter-mile champion, which means he has speed. But without me saying anything else, when he comes into your office, take a look at those huge hands of his."

So young Chuck Connors walked across Montague Street to see about becoming a baseball player. Impressing Rickey

As a Boston Celtic, Chuck Connors shattered a backboard.

with his own sincerity and appraisal of his ability, and bolstered by the Niss "scouting report," Chuck persuaded the Dodgers, who also had never seen him play, to produce a contract.

The bonus was set at $200 and the Dodgers prepared a check. "Wait a minute," protested Connors, who really didn't know what a check was in those days. "I don't want a check. You said you were going to give me $200."

Rickey and his aides laughed, but they sent a secretary down to the cashier to trade the check for two one-hundred dollar bills. Again Connors demurred. "No, I'm going to give the money to my mother and this really doesn't look like much. Could you give it to me all in one-dollar bills?"

So that was how Chuck took his bonus home to mom, the bills all scrunched up in a paper bag. When he got there, he exclaimed, "Hey, mom, look what I just got from the Dodgers to play baseball!" and he threw the bills up in the air like confetti.

Chuck's pro career didn't exactly start out with a bang. He was assigned to Newport, Arkansas, in the Class D Northeast Arkansas League and appeared in only four games and hit .091 before he broke his finger. The Dodgers sent him home, but continued to pay him his $65 a month salary, which was pretty good for Bay Ridge in 1940.

When he originally signed, Connors had told the Dodgers he wanted to go to college and he understood they had some kind of arrangement with Seton Hall in New Jersey. That fall, at the Dodgers' suggestion, he enrolled at Seton Hall. Despite the fact that he was technically a professional athlete, Chuck went out for the freshman basketball team. "I really didn't know. I was that naive. And when I enrolled, nobody asked me if I was a professional baseball player," Connors recalled.

Seton Hall had a great basketball team. The Pirates were working on a 43-game win streak led by Hall of Fame guard Bob Davies, and the freshmen were assigned to scrimmage the varsity. Honey Russell, the coach, says this is where Connors got his first acting job.

Participating in the National Invitation Tournament, undefeated Seton Hall was paired against powerful Rhode Island State. All week long, as he sharpened his strategy, Coach

Russell had Connors emulating the Rhode Island State center. But that was only part of the acting job. The freshmen also were instructed to keep the varsity fired up for the big game. Connors, with his mouth, was admirably suited for the job.

"Aaah, you big stiffs, no way you're going to beat Rhode Island State," Connors taunted. "Why, we're freshmen and we can beat you ourselves with one hand tied behind our back." Fights broke out regularly all week in practice and the varsity never caught on to how they were being psyched up. But the tactics worked. Seton Hall upset Rhode Island State in the first round before bowing in its next game to Long Island University.

During this period, Connors also was winning schoolwide elocution contests at Seton Hall, and he wrote a 19-stanza celebration of the school's great basketball team, which began:

Pause awhile, I pray you, and listen to my story
Muse a time, I beg you, upon this tale of glory
Concerning five young courtsters who, while they held their
    way
Meant more to old Setonia than sun means to the day.

Connors went on to play freshman baseball at Seton Hall that spring and in the summer performed in the Northern League for the Bennington (Vermont) Generals. This was supposed to be an amateur league for college players, and by now Chuck realized that general knowledge of his professional status could foul things up. He hit .329 and was the league's all-star first baseman. One of his biggest games, in which he hit three triples and a double, was attended by Paul Krichell, a famous scout for the New York Yankees.

Krichell approached Connors after the game, but Chuck brushed him off. "Oh, my father said I can't talk to anybody until I get out of school. Thanks very much, Mr. Krichell," Connors said as he hurried off. Krichell was shocked that anyone could turn down a possible Yankee offer so offhandedly.

The next winter, while Connors played varsity basketball at Seton Hall, his name appeared on a list of minor league players eligible to be drafted by other teams. The Dodgers, confident that they had Connors hidden because he hadn't played pro ball the previous season, did not bother to protect him by moving him up to a higher classification. Krichell's sharp eye spotted the name. Feeling pretty sure, as Connors tells it, "that there could not be two Kevin Joseph Aloysius Connors, 6-5½, left-handed first basemen, born in Brooklyn, who went to Seton Hall, he took a chance that I was the one he had seen play in the Northern League and drafted my name for the Yankees."

So, the next summer, after another spring of college baseball, Connors reported to the Yankees' Piedmont League farm team in Norfolk, Virginia, where he batted .264 with five home runs.

This was to be Chuck's last professional baseball season for quite a while. The next item in his scrapbook is a notation in his mother's neat hand: "Kevin left Brooklyn, N.Y., for Fort Knox to enlist in U.S. Army on October 11 at 6:30 P.M. 1942."

Connors' war career consisted mainly of basketball. He played on outstanding service teams at Fort Knox and West Point, and when he was stationed at the Military Academy he also played pro ball on weekends. When President Franklin D. Roosevelt died, he wrote a eulogy in verse that a soldier friend showed to the President's widow. The poem brought tears to Mrs. Roosevelt's eyes, and she invited Chuck over for lunch one day. But he was already booked for a basketball game and, at the time, the $25 for playing was very important.

Connors never returned to Seton Hall after his army duty. He moved right into professional basketball with the Rochester Royals of the old National Basketball League, who went on to win the 1946 NBL playoffs. In mid-March he reported for spring training with the Newark Bears, the Yankees' top farm team.

Chuck enjoyed a good training camp and thought he had the first base job won. But, at the last minute, the Yankees sent down a· more experienced man and prepared to demote Connors to a lower league. At this point, another technicality helped determine Connors' future. As a service veteran, Connors could not be farmed out unless he cleared waivers. That is, he could be farmed out only if no other major league team wanted him. But the Dodgers promptly claimed him right back for their No. 1 affiliate in Montreal. Connors spent two weeks there, playing with Jackie Robinson when the future Hall of Famer was breaking baseball's color line. Then Chuck was sent down to Newport News, Virginia, in the Piedmont League. The team was last when he arrived, but soon started moving and finished third and won the playoffs. Connors hit .293, 15 points higher than the team's young catcher, Gil Hodges.

When the baseball season ended, a new sports enterprise was in the process of starting. It was called the Basketball Association of America (forerunner of the National Basketball Association) and it was designed to provide true major league basketball for the first time in big city arenas. Boston had a franchise to be coached by Honey Russell, who sent for his old pupil, Chuck Connors.

Russell thought enough of Connors to offer him a no-cut contract for $5,000 that first season—quite good for those days—and the agreement included permission to leave early for baseball spring training with no loss in pay. (There was no danger of his deserting the team in the playoffs. The Celtics of that era were not good enough to make the playoffs.)

Despite his good contract, Connors' pro career was hardly distinguished. A good rebounder, he played in 49 games as a substitute that first year and averaged only 4.6 points. The following season he was released after four games in which he scored a total of only 12 points.

But Connors won fame for two bizarre incidents with the Celtics. In the first season, the new team was forced out of its home court, the Boston Gardens, because of a commitment to the rodeo. So the "home" opener was scheduled for the Boston Arena. It almost didn't come off. During pre-game warmups, a 30-foot shot by Connors shattered the glass backboard. Play was delayed until a replacement could be brought from the Gardens and Russell grumbled, "I should have left you in Newport News."

A year later, Russell had cause to be even more upset. The Celtics went into the last five seconds of a game in St. Louis with a five-point lead and possession of the ball. Russell called time out. "Don't let Connors handle the ball," he warned his players. But, as play was resumed, the referee blew his whistle and tossed the ball to Connors out of bounds. Chuck had no choice but to throw it in. The pass was intercepted, the player laid it in for a basket and then completed a three-point play when Connors fouled him. All in two seconds.

Now, three seconds remained, but the Celtics still led by two. Russell called another time out. *"Don't let Connors touch the ball!"* he screamed. Al Brightman took the ball out of bounds, but the Hawks were pressing. He could not find an open man. Connors came up court to help out. Brightman threw the ball to him, a Hawk cut in front to intercept, laid the ball in—and Connors fouled him again. Yes, Boston lost by one point.

The next morning in the lobby of the Chase Hotel in St. Louis, Connors was passing the time reading a volume of Shakespeare, when Russell came up behind him. "This guy loses me ball game after ball game and he sits here reading Shakespeare," Russell bellowed. "What have I got here, a ball player or a scholar?"

The question soon became unnecessary. Connors was released.

Chuck had done well at Mobile, Alabama, the previous baseball season and now began three years of success and frustration at Montreal. Batting averages of .307, .319 and .290, league championships and minor league World Series titles meant nothing as far as Connors' personal advancement was concerned. The mighty figure of Gil Hodges loomed ahead, and Connors realized he could not dislodge this man as the Dodgers' first baseman.

Although he got to bat once with the Dodgers as a pinch-hitter in 1949, Connors knew he was doomed to be a minor leaguer for the three seasons Brooklyn could safely option him out. Although he was the clown of Dodger spring training and served as master of ceremonies for the annual camp show, Connors cried inside. (Once Branch Rickey, Sr., offered to sell Connors to the old St. Louis Browns, but Connors, persuaded by the Dodger president that he could make more money at Montreal, short-sightedly turned the offer down. Montreal, after all, made the playoffs every year and Connors was drawing close to a major league salary.)

However, by 1951, Connors had no more options so Rickey sold him to the Cubs, who sent their new first baseman to Los Angeles, of the Pacific Coast League, to start the season. For the first two-thirds of the season, Connors hit .321 with 22 home runs, and the Cubs called him up. This was his big chance, at last, but he was already 30 years old. For the final 66 games in which he appeared, Connors hit .239 and two home runs, both of them in New York's Polo Grounds with his mother watching. But by then both Chuck and the pitchers had learned that he could not handle the major league high inside fast ball.

The next year he was back in Los Angeles, but this move couldn't have been to a better place or at a better time. When he returned from his brief spell at Chicago, a casting director who was a ball fan, called Chuck and asked if he'd like a small role in a movie. He'd heard of Connors' monologues and recitations and had been impressed by his antics on the ball field. Besides, it would be good publicity for the film; so Connors played a state trooper's role in a classic Tracy-Hepburn comedy, *Pat and Mike.*

"All I did was imitate Burt Lancaster and they gave me the part," Connors chuckles. But his big thrill was the chance to work with the late Spencer Tracy, and when someone asks Chuck for a definition of acting, he replies, "Acting is what Spencer Tracy did."

After the next season, Connors continued to get bit parts on his baseball reputation for more money than he ever dreamed one could come by honestly back in Bay Ridge. When he finally got a major role in an epic called *South Sea Woman*, he announced his retirement from baseball. (Everybody had to be tested for this picture, and Burt Lancaster, the star, made a rare appearance before Connors' test because he happened to be a baseball fan. When he saw that Connors wasn't up to the test and might lose the part, Lancaster ordered an hour's delay in the shooting and secretly coached Chuck so he could make good.)

The movie roles then began to come regularly, and Chuck was now a full-time professional actor. Then came television and starring roles in no less than four major series—*Branded,*

Cowboy in Africa, Arrest and Trial, and *The Rifleman.* He also served as host and narrator for a documentary series called *The Thrill Seekers.*

The Rifleman was the first and most popular of Connors' television roles and he is most often identified with that role.

"No, I don't mind that people still think of me as the 'Rifleman,'" Connors said one day in his home high in the north Los Angeles mountains. "It was a marvelous success and it ran for five years, all in the top ten. It was a good show, and it spoke for a family relationship, a man and his son. I think it had all positive values and any violence displayed in it was always shown to be bad, and hopefully, as being unnecessary in the future. It was a landmark in my life."

The series did create one personal problem, however. Connors has four sons and they were quite young at the time. He says it was most disturbing for them to see him on television with another "son." Schoolmates taunted the Connors boys by saying, "Aaah, he's not your father. He's got another kid on TV."

"I would bring Johnny Crawford, who played my son, over to the house and sleep him over so my boys would get to know him, but this was a trying period and I had to constantly reassure my own sons," Connors related.

In the 1970-71 season, the National Basketball Association celebrated its Silver Anniversary. Walter Kennedy, the NBA commissioner, had been the league's first publicity agent and he remembered a tall guy with a ready smile and wit to match. He further recalled that the fellow had been one of the league's original players. So he asked the now famous actor if he would serve as pro basketball's ambassador of good will through the anniversary season. Of course Chuck Connors agreed. As always, he was ready to play.

TENLEY ALBRIGHT
OF SKATES AND SCALPELS

THE YOUNG DOCTOR in the surgical gown peered intently at the gradually lessening wound. With deft, precise stitches, the freshly cut incision was closed and the early morning gall bladder operation was over.

"Neatly done," said the associate surgeon as he removed his surgical mask and gloves. On his way out of the operating room, he added, "See you at the office at two o'clock. You can make rounds and talk to the patient's husband."

The surgeon who had just completed the operation was Dr. Tenley Albright Gardiner, ex-Olympic figure-skating champion. A slender, beautiful blond mother of three little girls, she was in practice in Boston, Massachusetts, with her father, Dr. Hollis Albright.

So many different gowns for this 36-year-old woman to wear well, but Tenley passed with ease from one role to another, always performing with grace as well as perfection.

In one day, Dr. Albright could perform a delicate, painstaking operation, hold office hours, skate in an exhibition ice show, take one of her children to school or to some other activity, shop downtown, discuss the dinner menu with her

31

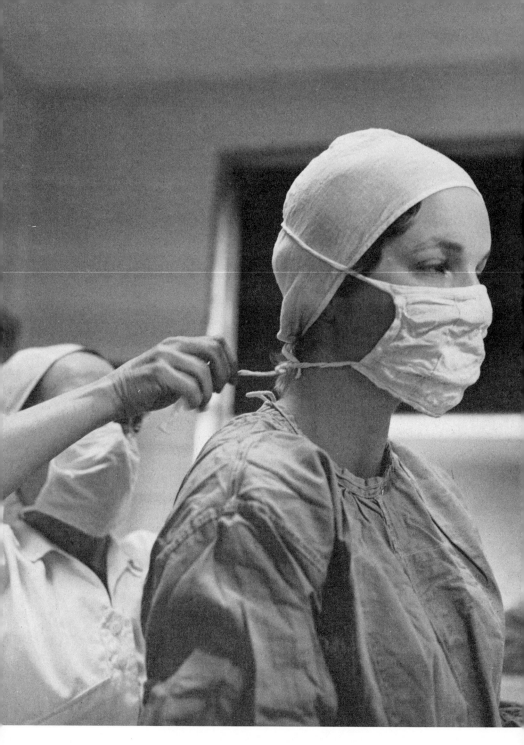

Dr. Albright gets ready for surgery.

housekeeper, and still have energy left to accompany her husband, Tudor, to the opening of a new play. And each phase of this whirlwind schedule was accomplished with poise and aplomb.

As a skilled surgeon, there is nothing typical about Dr. Albright. She is her own master in everything she does. Her strength is apparent but never overwhelming. She also exhibits the so-called old-fashioned virtues. She is soft-spoken, gentle, unassuming and kind. But she is always of steely purpose and whatever she does, she seems to do faultlessly.

Even as a little girl, Tenley was not one to take a mistake lightly. Once, in the first grade, she made a single error on a test paper; she did not capitalize the A in Albright. Tearfully, she went up to her teacher, Marion Proctor.

"I made a mistake," she sobbed.

"That's all right, dear," replied her understanding teacher, trying to cheer her up. "Everyone makes mistakes sometimes. You can always correct it on the other side of the paper."

"But," responded Tenley, feeling no better, "I still would have made the mistake."

Tenley's childhood was a happy one. She and her brother Nile grew up in the suburbs of Boston. The Albrights were prosperous, and the big clapboard and fieldstone house was filled with the signs of comfort and culture: books, music and interesting people. The family liked to be together and there radiated from them a feeling of warmth and understanding.

The Albright children were encouraged to follow their own inclinations. The development of both mind and body was considered important, and Tenley and Nile were allowed the pleasure of seeking their own fields of achievement, whether through active sport or mental stimulation.

Brother and sister were very close and even though Tenley was four years older, she respected Nile and treated him more like a "big brother." She was also much influenced by her Swedish grandmother, who cared a great deal about the world and people around her and passed this sense of duty on to her family.

In 1944, when Tenley was eight, she was taken to see six-time national figure skating champion, Gretchen Merrill, in an ice show. Tenley was enchanted and promptly asked her parents for ice skates. When the skates arrived under the tree at Christmastime, they turned out to be tubular with hockey blades instead of the notched figure type. It was difficult to keep from showing her disappointment, but by the time she started her lessons at the Skating Club of Boston, Tenley was full of eagerness to learn this new sport.

The club was so far from the Albrights' home that Tenley had to be driven there in one of the family cars. Since it was during World War II, gasoline for civilian use was restricted by rationing, and Tenley was allowed only one lesson a month. Her first teacher was the short, roly-poly Austrian champion, Willie Frick.

"He really made skating fun for me," she said. "Willie had such a great sense of humor. He would try to get me to laugh at my mistakes. He had some favorite comments to make whenever I fell down or goofed up. For example, he would say, 'Oops, the ice came up and hit you,' or 'Where there's still life, there's hope,' and somehow that always made me feel better."

These early lessons were very important to Tenley's development. Willie Frick's easy attitude toward learning and practice stayed with her, and later on, when the competition really got rough, she found that she was able to keep at her practice for long periods of time without getting discouraged.

In figure skating, more than in any other sport, perhaps, tedious practice is the essential ingredient for making a champion. Progress is made as a skater masters each of 67 school figures. A series of eight tests must be passed in order to officially record the successful mastery of these two- and three-lobed figures. It requires absolute precision, and the tracing and retracing of the figures is a boring process. More important, in competition you get only one chance to perform for the judges.

But Tenley rarely got bored or tired of skating. In between her lessons, if it was cold enough, she would practice in her own backyard, on a small pond which her father had had bulldozed for her.

Even in those days, Tenley was doing her own thing. Since few of her friends could ice-skate, most of the time she skated alone. But she didn't seem to care; she was not, as she would describe herself, much of a group person.

This ability to follow her own star grew stronger as Tenley grew older. Willie Frick said of her that she skated with her head and heart as well as her legs, and he certainly could not have predicted at that time in what varied directions Tenley's agile mind, generous heart and talented body would actually take her.

When Tenley was eleven, she was stricken by polio, which left so many children crippled and disabled. Fortunately, she had a mild case and coupled with her resoluteness, patience and grit, she was back on the ice in less than eight months. She worked with dogged perseverence at all the exercises prescribed and by the time she was skating again, her legs were almost back to normal strength.

That bout with polio made Tenley appreciate all the more the importance of good health and proper exercise. Being ill also gave her an intimate look at hospital routine and the dedication of the doctors and nurses who cared for her.

For the next decade, under the tutelage of Maribel Vinson, another champion skater, Tenley progressed steadily along the road laid out for competitive figure skaters. In addition, it was expected that she would also keep up with her studies. There was never any skating allowed until all her school work had been completed.

She set her own skating schedule, which called for practice from three to six hours a day. Even summers were spent on ice—first in Lake Placid, New York, and then in Denver, Colorado. Nobody ever had to coax Tenley. She was her own taskmaster.

Her first success came with the winning of the Eastern sectional title for juveniles under twelve, which she achieved less than a year after her polio siege. By 1952, when she was seventeen, Tenley made the U.S. Olympic team and went to Oslo, Norway, for the Winter Olympic Games. She won a silver medal. No other American woman had done as well since Beatrix Loughran took second place in 1924.

From then on, it seemed to be only firsts for Tenley. She became America's first winner of the World Championship in 1953, and that along with the U.S. and North American titles gave her this country's first triple crown winner.

That year too, as an 18-year-old, she was admitted to the

Tenley Albright won her Olympic gold medal at Cortina, Italy.

prestigious Radcliffe College in Cambridge, Massachusetts. She would get up when it was still dark and practice from four to six in the morning at the Boston Arena. Then there were ballet lessons, homework and study. It all added up to a grueling, exhausting schedule, but there was still not enough practice time for a competitive skater.

When Tenley returned to Oslo in 1954 to defend her world title, she went down in defeat, literally—after falling on the ice while executing the most difficult axel, double loop jump. It meant only a second place for her. What made it all the harder to take was the fact that an official had mistakenly notified her in the dressing room that she had won the gold medal again. As she burst into the arena to hear the announcement, the voice on the loudspeaker was calling Germany's Gundi Busch the winner!

A young person made of lesser stuff might have decided to give up skating at that moment. After all, Tenley had already achieved a triple slam, including a world crown, and she could certainly rest on these accomplishments. Also, she was particularly anxious to do well at Radcliffe, for she was already considering going on to medical school, and she would have to graduate at the top of her class to achieve that.

But Tenley was still a figure skating champion at heart, and with the help and encouragement of her coach, Maribel Vinson, she rescheduled her life with the primary goal the winning back of her world title.

Miss Vinson was impressed by Tenley's intense dedication to her plan. The pressure and hard work increased, but Tenley wasn't bothered by it. By the time the championships rolled around again, she was ready. Perhaps, as Miss Vinson suggested, one reason for Tenley's calm confidence this time was her knowledge that in contrast to the year before, she had spent enough time on the ice.

After a brilliant, error-free performance at the Wiener Eislauf Verein Stadium in Vienna, Tenley became a world champion once again. She followed this up by winning a gold medal in the 1956 Winter Olympics—the first such victory for an American woman.

But what did all this do to Tenley's ambition to be at the top of her Radcliffe class? Somehow her studies never suffered.

After only three years as an undergraduate, twenty-year-old Tenley was accepted at Harvard Medical School, one of six women in a class of 130. Now, becoming a doctor was her new passion.

Doctoring had been a part of her life ever since she was old enough to be aware of her father's comings and goings. Dr. Hollis Albright used to take his daughter to the hospital with him while he made rounds. There was no question but that Tenley would turn down the many elaborate offers to turn professional ice-skater in favor of medicine.

Once again, Tenley's life was one of work, practice and study, but this time it was within the confines of the school, hospital, library and home. There was little time for anything else, and often she was lucky to squeeze in a few hours of sleep at the end of a long day.

The same calmness and confidence that had pulled her through her crises on ice pulled her through this harrowing time of study. And once again she followed her own road. This time, after graduation from Harvard, Tenley chose a residency in surgery. There was only one other woman with the same ambition in her graduating class.

As a surgeon, Tenley soon discovered that she felt the same exhilaration from completing a good operation as she did when performing on ice. "It's like the theater," she said. "When things click, you get a very excited feeling." Her fulfillment comes from cancer surgery, gall bladder and thyroid operations and even occasionally from such lowly extractions as splinter removal. She prefers operating on women.

"I like doing things that require more precision than most," she explained. "Women don't like stitches to show too much and I want them to be happy with themselves. If I can do the job better than somebody else, that's really important to me."

Being a doctor satisfies two strong instincts for this gifted woman: that of loving people and that of loving challenge.

"I know," she commented, "that in this modern world people try to do things at their own pace to avoid pressure. In competition, as in surgery, of course, you can't do that. But it does make people work towards top performance and I think that's good."

As a mother, Dr. Albright tries to instill this strong sense of purpose and discipline in her children. Her little girls are taught to recognize what the limits are. She firmly believes that without guidance and rules, there can be no real freedom.

The Gardiner home reflects the kind of creativity that comes from this sort of freedom. The house itself sits high on a hill overlooking the city of Boston and the New England Baptist Hospital, where Tenley works. She and her husband planned their home themselves and it seems to sparkle not only with warmth and color but also with originality.

Tudor Gardiner, a six-foot, 220-pound lawyer, was a college wrestler and still loves to compete in the sport. Tenley is an avid spectator when Tudor has a match. Tudor is the only chairman of the New England Wrestling Association who graduated summa cum laude in classics from Harvard.

When Dr. Albright is with her children, Lilla, Elin and Elee, she tries to avoid the kind of attention that would single them out or cause them to fade in her shadow. She likes to keep in mind the time when she took her oldest daughter Lilla, who was then only five years old, to New York City. As a treat they went ice-skating at the Rockefeller Center rink. Tenley had a fine time skating, sometimes with Lilla and occasionally alone in the center of the ice. At the end of the session, Lilla came up to her mother and complained.

"You did so much twiddling around out there that I was embarrassed," she said.

In spite of all the big things the Gardiners have accomplished, the little things hold an important place in family life. Emphasis is still on liking what you are doing, and getting pleasure from doing for others.

On Valentine's Day one year, Tenley was awakened at 5:20 in the morning by her middle child Elin, who needed help in making a Valentine for Mor-Mor. (Mor-Mor means mother's mother in Swedish and refers to Tenley's mother.) Mor-Mor's own contribution to the children that day was a large heart-shaped rock, painted red, and left at the front door for one of her grandchildren to happen upon.

When Tenley is not busy being doctor, wife, or mother, she finds time for her own personal diversions. Occasionally she plays tennis with her brother Nile, skates for fun alone or gives impromptu lessons to the local children at the neighborhood rink. Her latest sport is bicycle riding. Once, after only a brief warmup period on the quiet streets around the house, Tenley and Lilla joined an American Youth Hostel group on a trip to Bermuda. There they bicycled an average of 25 miles a day for five days.

Tenley is a willing performer in ice exhibitions to raise money for the Figure-Skating Association Memorial Fund. The fund was established in 1961 after a tragic air crash in which 18 members of the U.S. Olympic figure-skating team were killed, including Tenley's former coach, Maribel Vinson.

Tenley wants to help get more young people out on the ice. Not just the rich ones, but anyone who has the will and the talent. One way to accomplish this is through group teaching at the public rinks, teaching which is sponsored by the fund. And she is one of the teachers.

"One can't just go through life without giving back to it," she says. "There is something bigger in this universe that can't be explained. When you give to it, that sort of gives you a proper perspective on the nature of things."

Dr. Tenley Albright has achieved a serenity about life that is unusual to find in this modern, complex world. "I realize," she once said, "that happiness is not something you set out to achieve. It's a byproduct of something you're doing."

BRUD HOLLAND
THE AMBASSADOR AND HIS FOOTBALL

It Was The fall of 1930 and the high school football team from Auburn, New York, was playing the team from East Syracuse. Auburn displayed an excellent freshman football player named Jerome "Brud" Holland who played fullback on offense and tackle on defense.

He seemed to be more than the usual freshman football player. First, he weighed 165 pounds. Second, his talent was developing. It was a close game that day, with the teams battling up and down the field but failing to score. With one minute to play, East Syracuse seemed to be driving for what could have been the winning touchdown.

The ball had been spotted on the Auburn 20-yard line when the East Syracuse quarterback went back to pass. Someone up front in the Auburn line blocked the pass and it squirted into the air. When it came down, it was cradled in the arms of Brud Holland, who took off down field and went 80 yards for a touchdown. When he crossed the goal line the stands emptied.

"There were about 30 seconds left," Brud Holland said, "but there were so many people on the field, the referee had to call the game."

As Ambassador, Dr. Holland got to know the Swedish people.

That marked the beginning of a lifetime of outstanding accomplishment for young Brud—in athletics and in public service.

Holland was born on January 9, 1916, in Auburn, a manufacturing town of about 35,000, including about 500 blacks. Most of the men worked in the shoe factory, the woolen mills, a steel forging plant, a rope company or at International Harvester's farm equipment facility.

Brud's dad, a gardener and handyman for the wealthy families of the city, was the father of 12 children. Half of them would die at early ages as a result of illness of one sort or another.

And young Jerome didn't escape early physical troubles. His legs were slightly deformed just below the knees. "My grandmother (Mrs. Julia Bagby) massaged my legs daily for more than a year, and eventually they became normal," he explained.

It was as a child that Jerome became "Brud." His three sisters called him "Brother," and the youngsters in the neighborhood, always ready with nicknames, shortened that to "Brud."

The Hollands lived in the southern end of town, known as the "Swamp Area." This was because a nearby creek would often overflow, creating a swamp, and though improvements were made over the years, it kept the name. The neighborhood consisted mainly of first generation Italian families as well as first generation Polish families. There also were some second generation Irish.

"You weren't conscious of racial prejudice as such," Holland said. "But you were conscious of race. There was the *Negro* church and the *Negro* fraternal orders, but the schools were integrated."

Brud attended the Genesee Street school, a ten-minute walk from the Holland house. There were no lunches in school; Brud walked home each day at noon. Few families had enough money for bicycles.

By the time Brud was ten he was growing strong and developing into a good athlete. He played baseball, football and basketball. On the diamond he was a pitcher, and one day he struck out 22 batters in a nine-inning game. The other team got a couple of hits, but Brud wasn't concerned about missing a no-hitter. He was satisfied to strike out so many batters.

For basketball, Brud and his friends used a peach basket with the bottom cut out—just as Dr. James Naismith had done when he invented the game of basketball in 1891.

Brud was a good student. "I always seemed to be in the 'B' range, with some 'B plusses,' " he said. But sports and schoolwork weren't the only things that occupied Brud. He did odd jobs helping his father, anything from sweeping sidewalks to shoveling snow. "I always had some kind of a job," he said.

Brud became serious about athletics when he began at Auburn High, where his memorable debut against East Syracuse was just a hint of what eventually would come in sports. He played in every high school football game for four years. Twice Brud broke his nose, once he suffered a bad cut over his eye, but there was no keeping him out of the lineup.

Meanwhile his teachers were encouraging him to work hard at school, to take the right subjects because they felt that he might be able to get a scholarship to college. "In our part of the country we were somewhat off the mainstream for the recruiters," Holland pointed out. "I was interested in getting into any school I could get into. They were not offering Negro boys scholarships."

A friend from the local YMCA took Holland to a meeting of some Cornell alumni, and the university in Ithaca, New York, 38 miles from Auburn, showed definite interest. They wanted Brud.

It wasn't that difficult a decision. Brud had ties with Ithaca. His father was a native of the town, having gone to Ithaca High School and played football on the city's south side. Coincidentally, Brud's grandfather had been caretaker at the residence of Andrew D. White, the first president of Cornell. This was the same Mr. White who did not favor his team's going any great distance to play and who once said, "I will not permit 30 men to travel 400 miles merely to agitate a bag of wind."

Brud had watched Cornell play a game when he was in high school. He and a few friends had hitched a ride to Ithaca and climbed the fence to get in. They didn't have the price of admission, or bus fare either.

Brud Holland, All-American end at Cornell.

Young Holland entered Cornell's School of Agriculture in the fall of 1935. As a freshman he had a full schedule on and off the field. To defray the cost of room and board, Brud took care of a coal-burning furnace in one fraternity house and worked as dishwasher-kitchen-boy-waiter in another. In the classroom he took three science courses—geology, physics and botany. And, of course, he was playing freshman football.

"I had to really study. You could flunk out without any difficulty, and I was determined to stay in school," Brud said.

In the summer following his freshman year, he worked on a farm in upstate New York. It was part of the School of Agriculture program. "I was up at dawn, beginning a day in which I would milk cows, spread manure, feed chickens, collect eggs, cut wheat. We were paid $20 a month."

The head coach at Cornell when Brud was a freshman was Gil Dobie, who decided to move the 200-pound Auburn lad from the backfield to end. When Brud came back as a sophomore there was a new coach, Carl Snavely, who agreed with Dobie. He told Holland, "You can tackle, you can block, you can run. You're too aggressive to be a halfback. Half the time you're up on the line tackling people. I think you can best capitalize on your natural abilities as an end."

Brud responded by being an instant success at his new position. As was the custom of the day, he played both offense and defense. Not only was he outstanding as a blocker and tackler, but he was the ball-carrier on Snavely's famous end-around play.

There was one game in 1937 against Cornell's arch-rival, Colgate, in which Colgate was the solid favorite. In each of the seven previous campaigns, Andy Kerr's teams hadn't given up more than a total of 40 points to their opponents.

Lloyd Scoville played opposite Holland as Colgate's right tackle. "The worst thing that could happen, did," Scoville said. "We scored right away on an easy pass play and figured we had an easy day ahead."

Colgate wasn't especially worried about Holland on the end-around. At least, not before the game. "We had practiced against it all week," Scoville explained. "We were ready. It was my job when I saw Holland swinging back, to yell, 'Here he comes, Red,' to Red Chesbro (Colgate's All-American nominee at the other defensive tackle spot). Being ready for Holland wasn't enough. The Cornell end-around was working perfectly that day. It started with fullback Kenny Brown bucking toward the line. Guard Sid Roth would pivot around and Brown would hand the ball to Roth, who would pitch a lateral to Holland.

Lloyd Scoville did a lot of yelling to Chesbro, but it didn't help. Holland scored three touchdowns in the last quarter and Cornell wound up with a 40-7 victory. Later in the year, Brud's contributions in the upset of Yale cemented his subsequent selection as an All-American.

Cornell, which had some lean seasons before Holland's arrival, finished with a 5-2-1 record in 1937. Then in 1938 came the big moment when the Big Red defeated Dartmouth for the Ivy League title, 14-7. For the second straight season, Brud Holland was All-American. Cornell finished 5-1-1.

But everything wasn't as rosy as it seemed when Brud's college career ended. "My grades," he said, "were considered good and I had been elected to the junior and senior honorary societies. I had been named left end on several All-American teams. In all modesty, I was recognized as an outstanding campus citizen.

"During the months before graduation, scores of industrial recruiters visited the Cornell campus. With a single exception, every member of the senior class who had compiled a record similar to mine was interviewed and offered one or more jobs. I was that exception. Nobody interviewed me. Nobody offered me a job. I was a Negro."

A professional career was out, too. "Pro football had the color line then," Holland noted. "I was about the only one among the senior regulars who wasn't drafted. There wasn't the money in pro football at that time that there is today and I never thought of it as a career. But I would like to have seen what I could have done in the pro game for a year or two."

From 1938 to 1942, Holland served as a sociology and physical education instructor at Lincoln University in Pennsylvania. Then he worked for a shipbuilding company during the remainder of World War II and later served as director of Political Social Sciences at Tennessee Agricultural and Industrial University from 1947 through 1951.

Dr. Holland and son Joseph visit iron mine in Sweden.

In 1953, he moved to Dover, Delaware, where he was president of Delaware State College. His master's degree came from Cornell in 1941 and his doctorate in sociology from the University of Pennsylvania in 1950.

Dr. Holland was named president of Hampton Institute in Virginia in 1960. He was considered in the tradition of famous Negro educators, including Booker T. Washington, Hampton's most distinguished graduate, who had opposed any attempts to overthrow American society and insisted instead that the Negro's best hope for economic advancement was to educate and train himself.

However, unlike Dr. Washington, who had seen little hope in civil rights, Dr. Holland demonstrated that he was a firm and outspoken integrationist and brought an increasing number of white students to Hampton's predominantly black campus.

In 1965, Dr. Holland, whose growing academic achievements had virtually obscured his identification with football, was named to the National Football Hall of Fame.

It was not his former activities on the gridiron, however, which prompted President Nixon to call Dr. Holland to the White House on January 12, 1970. "I would like you to go to Sweden to represent the United States as our ambassador," the President said.

Dr. Holland became Ambassador Holland.

The new ambassador knew that Sweden would not be an easy assignment for an American diplomat. There had been much opposition to U.S. foreign policy there, and Holland would have to try to smooth the relations between the two countries.

But he had been used to difficult situations. After all, he had been the first black to play football at Cornell, and he had been faced with bigotry for a good portion of his life. But through it all—and sometimes to the dismay of the younger generation he came in contact with on the college level—he called integration "my philosophy for living, as well as a practical reality."

"A United States Ambassador," according to the U.S. Government Organization Manual, "is the personal representative of the President and reports to him through the

Secretary of State. He has full responsibility for implementing the United States foreign policy by any and all United States Government personnel in his country of assignment, except those under military commands. The responsibilities include negotiating agreements between the United States and the host country, explaining and disseminating official United States policy, and maintaining cordial relations with that country's government and people."

During his appointment, the Ambassador made a number of visits back to the United States—to participate in State Department meetings, to attend sessions of Planned Parenthood, an organization of which he has been chairman, and to accept the Theodore Roosevelt Award from the National Collegiate Athletic Association. The "Teddy" goes to a former varsity college athlete who became "a distinguished citizen of national reputation and outstanding accomplishment."

Ambassador Holland wrote of his hopes for blacks and for the future of America in a book called *Black Opportunity*. Then, in May of 1972, he achieved another "first" when he was chosen the first black director of the New York Stock Exchange in its 180-year history.

Through everything, the Ambassador would smile when asked about his political ideas and theories. "I have studiously avoided telling anyone whether I am a Republican, a Democrat or a Socialist," he said.

But for a truer glimpse of the man, perhaps it is necessary to read the last paragraph of his book where he says, ". . . The only full solution (to the black problem in America) will come from people of goodwill of both races actively working together. This is the only way it can happen. For in the words of Edmund Burke, 'The only thing necessary for the triumph of evil is for good men to do nothing.' "

JIM BOUTON
THE ANNOUNCER IS A BULLDOG

THE GUEST LIST numbered Mickey Mantle and Bill Stafford, Yogi Berra and Johnny Kucks, Joe DiMaggio and Monte Pearson, New York Yankees big and small who had contributed to one of the team's 29 American League pennants. Jim Bouton, who won two games for the Yankees in the 1964 World Series, was not included.

"I understand why they did it," Bouton said, "but I couldn't let them get away with it completely." And so on July 10, 1971, Jim Bouton, pitcher, author and television sportscaster, appeared at Yankee Stadium for the annual Old Timers' Day, a charade of a game played among former Yankee stars.

Bouton didn't walk into the players' entrance as his former teammates were doing. Instead, he joined the line at a ticket window and bought a seat in the right-field bleachers. Bouton was the only 32-year-old on line wearing a baseball uniform. And viewers who tuned in to WABC-TV's Eyewitness News program the following Monday night were treated to the sight and sounds of Bouton mingling with other former Yankees—from a considerable distance.

"It's sure great to be back with the old gang," Bouton said

51

On the field or off, Jim Bouton cuts a sporting figure.

to the camera, an impish grin playing on his face. "Look at all the guys. Why, there's Mickey. Hey, Mickey!" And Bouton yelled at the top of his lungs to a muscular form 400 feet away. The muscular form didn't answer. The scene was unmistakably funny, unmistakably Bouton.

In a world where ex-athletes are paid to smile and say bland things about current athletes, Jim Bouton has made a significant impact. Just as he did with his best-selling book, *Ball Four,* which reduced baseball idols like Mantle to very human scale and hence earned the wrath of the sport's officialdom, Bouton has brought a bright, questioning mind and an irreverent sense of humor to his latest venture. "Sports is less than the most serious thing that ever happened," he said, and he labors five nights a week to prove it.

Bouton's office, a cluttered arrangement of three desks just off the main newsroom in WABC-TV's headquarters in New York City, reveals much about the man. On the wall there are pictures of his three children—Michael, Laurie and Kyong Jo, a Korean-American child whom the Boutons adopted in 1968—and a large poster of Charlie Brown, the cartoon patron of wishy-washiness, standing atop a pitcher's mound. "There's no heavier burden than a great potential," Charlie Brown is saying.

At the desk underneath the poster Bouton writes his daily scripts. Unlike most athletes who have succumbed to the lure of television, Bouton writes his own material. The material is never dry. "I told them when they hired me," he said, "I wanted to do anecdotes, editorials and features, not scores. They let me say what I want. I was lucky enough to come to a station desperate enough to want to change the way they did things."

The way Bouton did things was entertaining. He didn't just tell viewers about skiing, he showed them, leaving an imprint of his posterior all over a mountain in New Jersey. He played tennis against Arthur Ashe, charged into a "jam" at a roller derby much to his spine's surprise and, in his favorite fantasy, joined the rodeo. The sequence required him to jump into the barrel and play the clown, ride a reluctant horse and rope a calf. The calf was awarded a split decision.

"It's not news," Bouton said, "but people may get some

enjoyment out of it and at the same time learn some inside points about the sport."

A particularly brilliant piece emerged from a session with the New York University fencing team. After a brief, serious discussion with national champion Ruth White, Bouton donned a mask and immediately conjured up images of the Three Musketeers. In his own mind, of course.

Bouton dispatched each member of the team in turn until one masked swordsman remained. They parried and thrusted out of the room, down the hall, up a spiral staircase and into a waiting elevator. "Floor please?" the operator asked. "Lobby," Bouton replied, "and hurry."

The duel continued on the sidewalk, down the street and into a bar, the camera following with rapt attention. Finally, the beleaguered Bouton was trapped in a blind alley. He tried a door. And, as in all movie classics, the door was locked. His sword knocked from his hand, he stumbled to the ground. His adversary put a foot on his chest, the sword under his chin and removed his mask—her mask. It was Miss White, and Bouton lived to smile again.

"I got letters from people who follow fencing," he said, "and they said they'd never seen anything like it."

Bouton is not in the business just for laughs, although he'd be the last one to deny anyone a smile. "I think one of my shortcomings at first was I felt I had to pitch a no-hitter all the time," he said. "I don't think my approach is all that consistent now. The people don't really know what to expect from me."

A sensitive five-part series on playground basketball in Harlem displayed the other side of Bouton, who has a social conscience. Bouton has talked freely on his show about the plight of black athletes, the corruption of sports on the college and professional levels and the use of drugs. His guests have included Dave Meggysey, the football dropout who authored the book, *Out of Their League,* and Jack Scott, founder of the Institute for the Study of Sport and Society.

That is what Bouton calls his "heavy" material. "I think it's important that they remember me on roller skates or in the rodeo," he said. "That way they don't always feel offended when I have an editorial they don't agree with. They'll say,

Yankee Jim Bouton pitches against St. Louis in World Series.

'He's not a bad guy, he's entitled to his opinion.' It's better not to come on heavy all the time."

For all his forceful ideas and outspoken statements, Bouton's best vehicle is humor. On camera in the small studio which looks so much larger in the context of one's living room, Bouton's eyes appear to be perpetually crinkled in expectation of a future quip. In the next minute he might be doing his nasal imitation of the sonorous Howard Cosell, the melodramatic ABC-TV sports announcer, or launching a campaign to have viewers holler at professional golfers while they putt, or conducting a mad extemporaneous interview with Doug Rader, his former teammate on the Houston Astros.

In the course of one such interview Rader advised the youngsters watching that if they wanted to be major leaguers they would do well to eat bubble gum cards and thereby digest all the information contained on the back.

Nor is Bouton above making jokes at his own expense. The scene in Yankee Stadium was only one instance in which he assumed a less than heroic stance. In one of his very first interviews after assuming his TV spot in September, 1970, Bouton asked coach Weeb Ewbank, of the New York Jets football team, how a seemingly traditional coach could work with such a free spirit as his quarterback, Joe Namath. Ewbank answered the question and then, in an aside, said, "You're not going to get anywhere asking questions like that."

Bouton reported the conversation on the air, then said in his best little-boy manner, "When you're learning the business as I am, you're grateful for any suggestion."

That's Bouton's way with the news.

If there is such a thing as a natural athlete, Bouton wasn't it. He was the eldest of three brothers and the runt of the litter. "I was always the smallest kid in my class," he said.

What Bouton had was will power and a dream, a dream of someday wearing a major-league uniform. Even at an early age he demonstrated the tenacity which would later earn him the nickname, "Bulldog."

"I was a terrible kid," he said. "I always had to win. I got into fights. I was a poor sport. When I played football, I had to be quarterback. None of the kids liked me. I was a bad loser. I'd sulk, kick, cry and stomp. I was awful."

Bouton was born March 8, 1939, in Newark, N.J., and he did most of his kicking and stomping in a nearby suburb, Rochelle Park. The nicest thing about Rochelle Park was its proximity to the Polo Grounds, the playground of the New York Giants baseball team.

"I worshipped the Giants," he said, and he frequently led his brother Bob and several friends on expeditions to upper Manhattan. "We used to go early and sit in the upper left-field stands to catch fly balls during batting practice. We even conceived the idea of making a long fishing pole with a big net on the end of it to help us catch balls. We practiced with it for a week, throwing long fly balls to each other until we thought we had it down pat."

The big day finally arrived. "At first they wouldn't let us in with the pole," he said, "so we went around to another gate and sneaked it in. There were three of us and we held it at our sides underneath our coats and nonchalantly marched in." That alone made the day a success, which was fortunate because the net didn't catch a fly. "They didn't hit any our way," Bouton said, "but we had fun anyway."

Fun was yelling to the players for a nod of recognition, running the bases after the game and collecting as many autographs as possible on the day's scorecard. Almost as much fun was replaying the game the next day with the top half of a broomstick and a rubber ball. "You always wanted to be the hero of the game," Jim said. "I always wanted to be Willie Mays, but sometimes your brother wanted to be Willie Mays, too."

Bouton was sure his life was over at the tender age of 13 when his family moved to Chicago. In New Jersey they thought Jim Bouton was one fine baseball prospect. In Chicago they had never heard of him.

"I went to Bloom Township High School," Jim said. "There were 3400 kids there, a field house, a stadium. It was like a big college. I was lost. I couldn't even make the freshman-sophomore team. I had no name, no reputation. I weighed only 145 pounds. Here I was thinking I was going to be a big star and I didn't even pitch."

Bouton consoled himself with visits to Wrigley Field where he would root for his beloved Giants against the Cubs. "My brother and I sat behind their dugout," he said. "Everybody else razzed them, but we cheered for them. After I thought we had buttered them up enough, I asked Alvin Dark for his autograph. He told me, 'Take a hike, son.' "

Bouton's determination finally achieved a breakthrough in high school. After learning to throw off-speed pitches and developing a knuckleball from instructions on the back of a cereal box, he made the varsity as a senior. "I had to scrap for it," he said. "Actually, I think that's what made me a big-league ballplayer. If I had stayed in New Jersey and had it easy, I probably wouldn't have made it."

Bouton was all of five feet, 10 inches, and 150 pounds, at graduation, and no scouts were fighting over him. His father, George Bouton, a sales executive, steered him to Western Michigan University, where he displayed an intense interest in art and in a girl named Bobbie Heister. Miss Heister later became Mrs. Bouton.

It was during the summer following Bouton's freshman year at Western Michigan that he began to attract attention. He pitched two outstanding games in a Chicago amateur tournament and became a popular young man. The Yankees finally won a very mild bidding war with a $30,000 package, including his salary for the next three seasons.

Bouton celebrated his professional status by breaking the thumb on his pitching hand, and his first season in the minors was brief and ineffective. After two good years at Greensboro and Amarillo, Bouton landed in Yankee Stadium. He was no instant success, but he was instant refreshment.

The Yankees of that era had all the appeal of U.S. Steel. They were close-mouthed and defensive with no apparent zest for the game they played so well, and no appreciation of their fans. Bouton was different right from the beginning.

He did weird impersonations in the clubhouse. He enjoyed talking with fans and reporters. He offered candid opinions on everything from politics to religion. He actually had fun.

Bouton followed a mediocre 7-7 rookie season with a spectacular 21-7 in 1963. He clinched the American League pennant by beating the Minnesota Twins, and even a 1-0 loss to the Los Angeles Dodgers in his first World Series assignment couldn't ground his high spirits. He was "Bulldog" then,

Jim before he turned TV sports announcer

a tough young man who put so much effort into his pitches that he frequently spun out from under his cap.

The high point of his career came in 1964. After finishing the season with an 18-13 record, Bouton started and won the third and sixth games of the World Series against the St. Louis Cardinals. He savored the moment as only one could who had sat in the left-field stands and dared to dream.

"It's all that they could want it to be," he said, referring to the future Jim Boutons in the stands. And he told the people who inquired, "I feel sorry that all you guys can't share in this feeling I have."

It was downhill from there. A sore arm robbed him of his fastball, and Bouton labored to hang on. The Yankees demoted him to the International League for a part of the 1967 season and in 1968 they gave up on the "Bulldog," selling him to Seattle of the Pacific Coast League. In desperation, Bouton turned to the knuckleball he hadn't used since high school and made it back to the majors in 1969 with the Seattle Pilots, a first-year expansion club in the American League.

That season, his last full year in baseball, was the framework for the book, *Ball Four*. He collected notes all season, preserving them on tape, capturing the insiders' sights and sounds of baseball as he fluttered, like his knuckleball, from Seattle to Vancouver in the Pacific Coast League, back to Seattle and into the midst of the National League pennant race with the Astros.

"I did the book," Bouton said, "because I wanted to entertain people, and I did it because I wanted some things told from the inside, like how general managers cheat players, and because—let's not kid ourselves—I wanted to make some money. But mostly I did it because I wanted to go down in history as the guy who wrote the book you absolutely have to read if you want to understand something about this American subculture called baseball."

There were cries of foul when excerpts from the book appeared in *Look Magazine* in June, 1970. He was termed a "social leper" by one baseball writer for violating the so-called sanctuary of the clubhouse embodied in the familiar sign: "What you see here, what you hear here, let it stay here, when you leave here."

The book was so outspoken it stung, and among those wounded was Mickey Mantle. For many officials of the game, that was the unkindest cut, picturing a superstar as something less than a superperson. "Let kids start thinking about some real heroes instead of phony heroes," Bouton replied. "Baseball is strong enough to withstand an inside look."

Among those who feared for the game's safety was the Baseball Commissioner, Bowie Kuhn. Bouton, still on the Houston roster at the time, was summoned to the Commissioner's office and censured. The meeting had the exact opposite of the desired effect. Bouton became an instant celebrity and his publisher doubled the size of the book's first printing. The fact is, rather than harm baseball, the book enlivened it, capturing at the same time the beauty and insanity which make it worthy of our attention.

Bouton, whose knuckleball was not doing very well, was demoted to the minors. Soon thereafter he announced his retirement. At the conclusion of *Ball Four* he recalled a conversation he had with a Cincinnati cab driver near the end of the 1969 season. The cab driver told him that Jim O'Toole, who had been at spring training with Bouton only that season, was pitching for the Ross Eversoles team in the Kentucky Industrial League.

"Then I thought, would I do that?" Bouton wondered aloud. "When it's over for me, would I be hanging on with the Ross Eversoles? I went down deep and the answer I came up with was yes.

"Yes, I would. You see, you spend a good piece of your life gripping a baseball and in the end it turns out that it was the other way around all the time."

And so Jim Bouton, 32, became a pitcher again in 1971 with the Ridgewood-Paramus Barons, a semi-pro team from his neighborhood in New Jersey. Not only did he have fun, but he had something to say to his viewers. What he said sounded distinctly like, "The kid is making a comeback."

Bob Pettit on the job at the Jefferson Bank and Trust Co.

BOB
PETTIT
FROM BASKETS TO THE BOARD

BOB PETTIT SAT behind a huge polished wooden desk, shuffled his feet on the thick carpet and looked up with a startled expression on his face as a visitor said, "Mr. Chairman of the Board—"

"It's still Bob," he interrupted.

Bob Pettit wasn't used to being called Mr. Chairman yet, even though he *was* Chairman of the Board of the Jefferson National Bank and Trust Company of New Orleans. Robert E. Lee Pettit, Jr., was a banker, all right, and a very good one. But to his friends, he was still Bob, Bob Pettit, one of the greatest players in the history of the National Basketball Association.

Pettit, of course, didn't start out as chairman of the board of a bank, and he didn't start out being a great basketball player either. In fact, he was not much of an athlete when he started playing.

He stood 5-foot-7 and weighed 118 pounds when he entered Baton Rouge High School in Louisiana. He tried out for the football team.

"At fourteen, I had more of a figure than a build," Bob

63

said. "They put me on the squad as a third-string tackle. I was
sent in for one game as a right tackle instead, and they went
right through where I was supposed to be for a 65-yard
touchdown. That ended my football career."

He tried baseball. "I got to play second base this one time,"
he remembered, "and the guy hit a ball to me and it went right
through my legs. That ended my baseball career."

And he tried basketball. At least he qualified for the junior
varsity team. But the season of his freshman year was hardly a
triumph. Pettit was the last player on the team, and he
managed to go through the entire schedule without scoring a
single point. Fortunately, that did not end his basketball
career.

Bob may have been disappointed that first year, but as a
sophomore it was even worse. He couldn't even make the 12-
man varsity squad. This setback brought out the extra drive
and determination that would be a Pettit trademark all his life.
He wouldn't be satisfied until he had earned the right to wear
the green sweater with the proud gold letters of Baton Rouge
High.

"When I look back," he said later, "the greatest thing that
ever happened to me was that when I first picked up a
basketball, I was terrible. If things come naturally, you may
not bother to work at improving them and you can fall short of
your potential."

The first step on his road to self-improvement occurred in
church. With the help of Reverend Philip Werlein, pastor of
St. James Episcopal Church, Bob Pettit and several other
youngsters formed a three-team church league. The games
weren't very well organized and the boys played with
something less than amazing grace, but it was a start.

His confidence bolstered by his status as a regular on the
church team, Bob began dreaming of that letter again.
Practice would help. He bent a wire coat hanger to simulate a
basket, hung it over the garage door and spent hours pepper-
ing it with tennis balls.

Eventually, the senior Pettit got the message. Bob's father, a
rugged man who stood 6-foot-4, had played basketball at
Westminster College before the first World War, and he was
pleased with his son's interest in the game. The wire coat

hanger soon was replaced by a regulation backboard and hoop, and the tennis balls gave way to a regulation basketball.

For the next three years Bob Pettit rarely strayed from his driveway. While in high school, he averaged three hours a day on the improvised family basketball court. He practiced in summer, winter, spring and fall, and not even darkness interfered with the routine. Bob placed two lamps on the windowsills facing the backyard and kept right on shooting.

His mechanical development was slow and painstaking. Not so his physical development. At the end of his sophomore year he was just shy of six feet. By the time he reported back to school he was up to six feet, four inches.

His quick growth, combined with a six-week program at a boys' basketball camp, gave Bob a new status. Suddenly, he was someone to be respected.

As the tallest player on the squad, Pettit was shifted to center. He was still skinny, but constant exercising had given him the strength to hold his own under the boards. Bob averaged 14 points that season, including a game high of 32, and at last gained possession of the green-and-gold sweater.

When he grew nearly three more inches the following summer, it was clear that Bob Pettit was destined for greater achievements. He starred as Baton Rouge won eight of its first eleven games, then the team lost nine in a row. There was a good reason. Bob was sidelined by the mumps.

Upon his return, however, Baton Rouge swept into the state tournament and won the championship. Pettit had led the team to seventeen consecutive victories, and his individual excellence earned him a spot on the South team for the North-South All-Star high school game in Murray, Kentucky. Almost suddenly, it seemed, Bob was a star.

Although fourteen schools showed sufficient interest to offer a basketball scholarship to Pettit, he had long since made up his mind. He wanted to stay at home and attend Louisiana State University. Naturally, coach Harry Rabenhorst was delighted.

The Bob Pettit who walked onto the campus in September, 1950, was a far cry from the shy, awkward youngster who had failed to make the high school team only three years earlier. He had grown to 6-foot-8 now, and before he had played even one game of basketball for the Tigers he was a celebrity.

There was no tradition of excellence in LSU basketball, so Pettit created one. As a freshman he averaged better than 30 points per game and his team won eight of ten. The step up to the varsity didn't slow him at all. His average of 25.5 as a sophomore was the third best in the nation behind Clyde Lovellette of Kansas and Dick Groat of Duke, both seniors, and LSU went 17-7, losing a playoff for the Southeastern Conference championship to Kentucky by one point.

As much as basketball meant to him, he always had an eye for the future. While other athletes sailed through their courses at Louisiana State University, Pettit took more than a passing interest in his studies in the School of Business Administration. And while other students loafed away the summers, Bob went to work in his family's real estate agency.

"You can only go as far as you're willing to work," he said. And he was willing to work very hard indeed.

The Tigers reached the NCAA tournament in each of Pettit's last two seasons, and the team's success was no mystery. In his junior year Bob averaged 24.7 points and in his senior year he outdid himself. Pettit scored 46 points against Georgia Tech, 50 points against Georgia and 60 points against Louisiana College in a torrid race with Furman's Frank Selvy for national honors. With a month left in the season it was too close to call. But Selvy singlehandedly scored 100 points against Newberry and ran away with the title. Selvy finished with a 41.7 average, breaking all collegiate records. Pettit's runner-up 31.7 was remarkable in its own right.

The National Basketball Association draft followed the scoring charts. The Baltimore Bullets, choosing first, grabbed Selvy. The Milwaukee Hawks, choosing second, picked Pettit.

The Hawks didn't have many good ball players, but then they didn't have many fans, either. All anyone in town seemed to care about was the new baseball team, the Braves. Naturally, Ben Kerner, the Hawks' owner, was in no position to offer his prize catch the key to the city.

"He offered me $11,000," Pettit said. "I wanted $15,000. I got $11,000." It was the last time Bob ever came up short on a business transaction.

Coach Red Holzman took one look at the 6-foot-9, 205-

pound beanpole and decided he wouldn't survive more than a minute at center in the NBA. From that time on, it was Bob Pettit, forward.

Pettit was not exactly an instant sensation. The Hawks, it so happened, had scheduled a series of ten exhibition games against the champion Minneapolis Lakers, and the first of these meetings occurred in the high school gym in a small town called Wolf Point, Montana. Pettit's first recollection of the Lakers was their size—George Mikan, 6-10, 275 pounds; Clyde Lovellette, 6-9, 245; and Vern Mikkelsen, 6-7, 255. Mikkelsen was the fiercest looking of the three.

In the first half, Holzman's worst fears were realized. Mikkelsen mauled the rookie, pushing him up and down the court at will. "Tell me, Pettit," Holzman asked Bob at halftime, "do you like playing professional basketball?"

"Yes, sir," Pettit replied. "I think it's fine."

"Well, then, let me tell you something," Holzman said. "If you don't go out there and hit the first guy you see coming at you, I'm going to ship you back to Baton Rouge tomorrow."

Pettit tried very hard not to look at Mikkelsen as the second half started. Fortunately, the Hawks won the tap and the ball came in to Pettit at the high post. Teammate Bob Harrison cut by him with defender Slater Martin a half-step behind. Martin, the Lakers' veteran guard, was 5-10 and weighed all of 165 pounds. Now here was someone Bob could handle.

No sooner had Pettit swung his elbow at Martin than Martin was gone. The elbow did land, but on the massive chest of the scowling Mikkelsen, planted behind him. For the longest time Pettit stood there, not knowing what to do or say. Finally, he looked Mikkelsen in the eye and said sheepishly, "Please excuse me, Mr. Mikkelsen."

But Pettit learned from his harrowing experiences, and soon he was able to cope with the league's tough guys. In the course of his career, Pettit would have 125 stitches taken in his face and suffer two broken arms, four broken bones in his back and a damaged knee. But he gave as good as he got, and he never again had to say, "Excuse me," on the court.

Bob averaged 20.4 points per game that first season, the fourth best mark in the league, and he was honored as the NBA's Rookie of the Year. The Hawks celebrated by moving

Bob Pettit shoots against Boston's Bill Russell.

to St. Louis. And Bob got a raise in pay. But the signing of a professional contract hardly satisfied Pettit's financial ambitions. If anything, it whetted them.

In the off-season he studied insurance and soon formed his own insurance agency. He called on his real estate background and went into partnership in a land development company. He never took a summer off. And all the while, of course, he was proving himself one of the great stars in the history of basketball.

Pettit and the Hawks rose to new heights in their new home. Within one year, Bob was the leading scorer and rebounder in the NBA. Within two years, the Hawks were playing the Boston Celtics for the championship.

Pettit broke his left wrist in January of that second season in St. Louis, yet missed only one game. Playing with a specially designed cast, he averaged 29.8 points a game in the playoffs and led the surprising Hawks into the finals. The Celtics prevailed, but the Hawks took them into double overtime of the seventh game before the issue was settled.

There was no stopping the Hawks the following season despite another broken bone suffered by Pettit, this one in his left hand. Again, a cast was designed. Bob missed two games this time around. St. Louis won its division easily, brushed past the Lakers in the semifinals and prepared once again to meet the Celtics.

The Celtics, with the arrival of Bill Russell at center, had been fashioning a dynasty. But the Hawks took a 3-2 lead in games in the four-of-seven series.

The sixth game was played in St. Louis. The lead seemed to change with each tick of the scoreboard clock. First the Celtics would be on top, then the Hawks, back and forth into the final quarter. The Hawks led by just one point, 108-107, but Pettit put the game and the championship on ice with a jump shot in the last 15 seconds. In the 110-109 victory, Bob scored 50 points, including 19 of his team's last 21.

Off the court, too, Bob kept looking for new worlds to conquer. In the fall of 1962, a call from Clifford Ourso, President and Chairman of the Board of the American Bank and Trust Company of Baton Rouge, prompted an important decision in Pettit's life. Ourso offered Pettit a position with the bank. "For the first time I had an offer which really appealed to me," he said, "so much so, I began thinking of retiring from basketball."

But Bob was only 29, still in his prime, and reluctant to leave the game at that age. "Bob," Ourso said, "you can work here six months a year in the off-season and learn all about the business." The two men shook on that.

Pettit worked at the bank after the 1962-63 season and knew that this was what he wanted. "I never wanted to make a career of basketball," he said. "I was more interested in the business world. I felt I was marking time in basketball."

He went to Ben Kerner, owner of the St. Louis Hawks and a close personal friend, before the start of the 1963-64 season, and told him he would play two more seasons.

Pettit maintained his excellent play. The Hawks never won another championship but it wasn't for Bob's lack of effort. He made the All-Star team every season and, in all, he four times won Most Valuable Player honors in that game. On February 8, 1964, he scored his 19,204th point, breaking the all-time career record held by Dolph Schayes. On November 13, 1964, Bob became the first man in the history of the game to score more than 20,000 points. For the record, it was a seven-foot hook shot against the Cincinnati Royals. He finished the season with a total of 20,880 points as a professional, a total only five other men have reached.

"After that," he said, "there was nothing else for me in the game." And Bob Pettit left it at age thirty-three, with what probably would have been two more lucrative seasons ahead. He had decided to accept the position at the American Bank and Trust Company. He was Vice President in charge of business and industrial development, a big title but at about one-fifth of his annual basketball salary.

He left basketball because, he said, "I could tell I was beginning to slip and I wanted to retire while I was on top." He then plunged into his new career. He attended the School of Banking of the South, and later served on the boards of several banks before becoming Chairman of the Board at the Jefferson Bank in December, 1970.

The same competitive drive which had carried him to the top in basketball also carried him to the top in business.

ALEX KROLL
HE ROSE ON "THE WINGS OF MAN"

"Keep Your Knees apart," father ordered as he rolled a ball across the living room floor to his infant son. This is Alex Kroll's first memory. Even as a toddler, there were sports; and there was the command to do it right.

Do it right; pay the price; success means praise. These maxims would pay off through a lifetime, on and off the field.

Father was a baseball player. A third baseman and manager of one of the many semi-professional teams in the steel mill and coal mining valleys of western Pennsylvania. Father was also a steel worker. He was thirty-three years old when his first child, Alex, was born and by the time the lad was three, they had graduated from the living room for their ball playing. In warm weather, father would return from his job at the mill, hot, grimy and fatigued, take a cooling drink and then haul himself to his feet. "All right, Alex, let's hit a few ground balls," he'd say and the day's ritual would begin.

Football, however, would eventually be the game for Alex Kroll. Football was more than a sport in western Pennsylvania, it was almost a religious rite. By the time he was eight, Alex had vowed, "Someday I'm going to be an All-

71

Alex Kroll achieved All-American honors at Rutgers.

American." In this fantasy, he was always a running back, dashing and skipping down field on fancy touchdown runs. His team? Notre Dame.

In autumns to come, the Krolls, father and son, often drove to Pitt Stadium to watch the University of Pittsburgh play. Even from their seats in the end zone, the glamor of the game, the color and the noise, had a profound effect on young Alex. "It was so very romantic and unpainful," Kroll recalls now in his office on New York's Madison Avenue.

Madison Avenue is the Main Street of the advertising business, and Alex Kroll, if not one of the kings of the industry,. is at least a crown prince with Young & Rubicam, the world's second largest advertising agency. Young & Rubicam has 3,800 employees in twenty-one offices around the world. Kroll's official title is executive vice president and creative director, which means he is second only to the agency's president, and he has to approve all of the creative advertising the company prepares. He was named to this position at the age of thirty-three.

Leechburg, Pennsylvania, Alex Kroll's home town, is 28 miles northeast of Pittsburgh. It is gray, drab. Once there was a steel mill and a coal mine, but now the mine is closed down and the young people go elsewhere, as Alex did, to make their way. When Alex was growing up, the population was 3,500. It is less now. In the foothills of Appalachia, "hillbilly and Slavic culture convene," Alex says with the flair for a colorful phrase that explains his success in advertising.

Kroll's father, also named Alex, came from a family of thirteen children and had to quit school after the fourth grade to go to work. Kroll's mother had gone through ninth grade.

About the only thing that stamped the Krolls as unusual was the father's custom of chartering small airplanes to take the family on trips whenever he had saved up a few dollars. The journeys were to quite ordinary places like Detroit and Schenectady, but the elder Kroll apparently was able to invest them with some glamor. Many years later, in the "Wings of Man" commercials which Young & Rubicam prepared for Eastern Airlines, the actor extolling the virtues of our American cities is really using the words of Mr. Kroll as he talked to Alex and his brother on those family excursions.

Kroll's middle name is Stanley, in honor of the great baseball player, Stan Musial, and baseball was where Alex's career in organized athletics began at the age of twelve. All those long hours of picking up ground balls—"Knees apart!"—paid off. Young Alex, playing second base sometimes on teams with men twice his age, could really field.

However, despite his father's dreams, Alex soon turned to football. To be accepted by his peers, he had to go out for the team because football was everything in Leechburg. Some games drew 7,000 fans, twice the town's population. To Alex, it was not surprising that the new Catholic church was built right next to the football field, a manicured oasis of green that seemed truly to be holy ground.

Kroll, thirteen years old, was not a very imposing figure when he showed up for his football practice as a Leechburg High School freshman. He was only 5-foot-6 and weighed a mere 114 pounds. The only thing big about him was his feet, size 10, and the equipment manager issued him a pair of size 13 shoes. That was all they had left for him.

The first day was almost Alex's last when over 100 candidates for the team gathered on an all-dirt practice field on a steamy August morning.

Kroll immediately showed the enterprise that would help him all through life. He knew that in the crowd of aspiring football players there was only one center. This lad was a junior, and he was quite small. The coach had to carry at least two men for each position, so that is how and why Alex Kroll decided to become a center.

However, in his calculations, Alex failed to consider that Leechburg High also took in students who had attended primary schools out in the county or rural areas. His jaw dropped, his hopes seemed doomed when out to join the centers strolled a confident newcomer from one of the area farms—big, fast, heavily muscled—and sixteen years old!

The coach had his own way of cutting the squad that first day. He started them with a mile-run around the track, then, when they thought the ordeal was over, he added another lap. Following this came 45 long minutes of calisthenics, then a series of wind sprints by position; the backs together, the ends together, etc. There would be ten of these, he announced, of 100 yards each.

As Alex drove himself through these sprints, unconscious of any feeling but pain, he knew he would not last. It would be a disgrace to drop out, his numbed brain reasoned, and so he would become a priest. The Church was one place where he could hide from this humiliation.

But he plodded on anyway, 100 yards on 100 yards. And on the eighth sprint, so close to the end, the big farm kid who had seemed so strong gave up and walked off the field. Alex somehow managed to run the two final sprints and survived to make the team. The triumph wasn't exactly complete, however. Through his freshman year he appeared in very few games, but he was allowed to scrimmage against the varsity every day. It was a rugged indoctrination.

That summer Alex vowed he would never again be subjected to such one-sided punishment. With money saved from his paper route, he bought a $13 set of 70-pound York bar bells by mail. All during his vacation he worked out twice a day, religiously. During the day, he'd practice in his room and every time he dropped the weights, dirt would filter through the ceiling into his mother's kitchen. She yelled louder than the coach. His second workout took place in the middle of the night. He would wake himself at 3:30 in the morning and haul the weights down to the kitchen where he could work without disturbing anybody. These sessions lasted two hours—when he didn't fall asleep between lifts.

The weight-lifting, the running that he did and the simple process of growing up made a miracle. When he returned to school in the fall he weighed 155 pounds. At last he could hold his own physically. He weighed 175 pounds as a junior and 205 pounds his senior year. The Leechburg Blue Devils were undefeated in Kroll's junior season and that was when his game started coming together. He was a devastating blocker on offense and an outstanding tackler at linebacker on defense. He made all-Western Pennsylvania at both positions.

To top it all, he also developed into an outstanding student, making almost all A's and graduating with the second highest average in his class. Offers of college scholarships came pouring into the Kroll household.

However, as he pondered the offers—many of them including new cars, wardrobes, spending money—Alex was disturbed. Somehow Yale University had overlooked him. So, with characteristic aggressiveness, he wrote Yale a letter telling the Elis what a good bet they were overlooking.

It wasn't too long before a member of the Yale Club in Pittsburgh was knocking at the Kroll door. Within days, Alex was on his way to visit the campus. He had written the letter solely out of wounded pride. He had no feeling about Yale one way or the other. But the more he saw of the school, its traditions, campus and academic program, the more he liked it. The football team was pretty good, too. Yes, Yale it would be.

His first year, Kroll made the Dean's List and was named co-captain of the freshman team. The next season he became one of only two sophomore regulars and, as for the first time he trotted out onto the hallowed turf of the Yale Bowl, he felt that at last he had recaptured the excitement of those childhood days with his dad in Pitt Stadium.

With sophomore Kroll calling defensive signals and playing each game at center and linebacker in an emotional frenzy, Yale rolled to an 8-1 record, losing only to Colgate this season of 1956.

Alex Kroll was a happy young man living in the best of all possible worlds of sports and academia. Suddenly, these worlds were destroyed. It was spring, vacation only three weeks away, and Alex was involved in a minor automobile accident. There were words between Kroll and the other driver, an older man. Kroll threw a punch and sent the other man flying with a broken jaw. The punch also knocked Alex out of Yale. The man was an associate professor. Kroll was told he could finish up the term if he moved off campus to the local YMCA, but after that he would be expelled. Perhaps in another year or so he could apply for readmittance.

Crushed, Kroll joined the Army. Later, when he learned that Yale had no intention of taking him back, he decided he would remain in the Service, playing on Army teams until he became eligible to turn professional. There seemed to be no alternative.

However, Art Robinson, a teammate and one of the officers

at Fort Campbell, Kentucky, had played football at Rutgers University in New Jersey. Just before Kroll re-enlisted, Robinson persuaded him to try once more to return to college, and he arranged an interview at his own alma mater. "If you mess up here, it's the end of the road," Kroll was told as the school almost grudgingly admitted him without scholarship. He then sat out the next season until he became eligible as a transfer student.

The following summer, Kroll's old intensity toward football began to return. He resumed his high school regimen of pre-dawn weight-lifting. He ran several miles each day. His weight moved back up to 230 pounds, which had been his playing level at Yale. The obsession to make All-American was still there. "This is my last shot," he told himself, fully aware even then that it takes a two-year buildup to make the cherished All-American lists.

Kroll gave Rutgers something to advertise as he made All-East while leading the Scarlet Knights to an 8-1 record. Elected captain for the following season, he stood up at the annual team banquet and vowed that he would return to school (he could have turned pro) and lead Rutgers to its first undefeated record.

Kroll spent that summer as a counselor at a camp run by Rutgers coach John Bateman. Despite a bad back (cured by an osteopath), Kroll worked out on the beach at night as campers played Princeton's fight song to psych him on. He showed game films to his campers. And he sent postcards to team-mates all summer, urging them to be ready for the opening game against Princeton, Rutgers' arch rival.

The Knights were tense as they came out on the field of Princeton's Palmer Stadium for the opening game. "Even the grass was hostile," Kroll recalls. But the Knights held on for a 16-13 victory.

After this, it got easier. One opponent after another tumbled before Rutgers, which made the "quarterback sneak" one of its big plays behind Kroll's steamroller blocking. Going into its final game against Columbia, Rutgers had an 8-0 record. But the Lions had a three-game winning streak and already had clinched a share of the title in their conference, the Ivy League. More than 25,000 fans jammed every vacant spot in Rutgers Stadium, many of them unwittingly camped in patches of poison ivy in the open end of the field.

Rutgers jumped off to a 7-3 lead, but then the Lions rallied to go in front by 19-7 entering the final period. Rutgers and Princeton had played the first college football game back in 1869, and in all that time the Knights had never enjoyed an undefeated season. Now it appeared that they never would.

But on the first play of the final quarter, quarterback Bill Speranza passed for a touchdown and on the next series, following a Rutgers interception, he sneaked into the end zone for another score behind a massive block by Kroll. Both times the Knights made two-point conversions and the score was tied. Continuing to dominate their foes, the Knights scored twice more for a 32-19 victory that assured the perfect season.

And Alex Kroll achieved his childhood dream. He made All-America. His scholastic record was no less impressive, and he was elected to the national academic fraternity of Phi Beta Kappa.

These weren't the only milestones for Alex Kroll. During the football season—right after one of the nine victories—he became engaged to Phyllis Benford, his home town sweetheart, whose father owned the steel mill back in Leechburg. They were married in Miami on the eve of the North-South game and honeymooned while Kroll appeared in other All-Star contests. Now Alex really had to ponder his future. Almost twenty-five, he was older than most of his classmates.

At one time Kroll had thought of attending law school, but now he felt his future was in the field of advertising. He had offers from the Los Angeles Rams, of the National Football League, and from the New York Titans, of the newer American Football League. The Titans of 1962 were a highly unstable franchise. They had never, in three years, signed a single high draft choice, but a Rutgers alumnus, David A. (Sonny) Werblin, gave Kroll this advice: "I know the money and the football future won't be the same as with the Rams, but if you want to get into advertising, stay in New York. Sign with the Titans."

Kroll took Werblin's advice. But there were times when he wondered if he had done the right thing. The Titans were a collection of battle-worn veterans who resented all rookies and took it out on Kroll because he was the only rookie around to resent. Kroll's extreme self-confidence didn't make things any easier for him. "I meant to break his arm," a defensive tackle complained after being told he had broken a bone in Alex's hand.

The Titans were a disaster. They carried only a bare minimum of players, and Kroll, expected to be a second-string center, soon found himself pressed into service as a starting tackle. Not heavy enough for pro football to start with, Kroll soon wore down to a scrawny 219 pounds and billed himself as "the lightest tackle in pro football." Nobody coached him in the techniques of the new position. By mid-season, the team went bankrupt and payroll checks bounced—in other words, the players were playing for nothing.

In his final game of the season, already disillusioned with life as a professional, Kroll suffered the fourteenth concussion of his long football career. When his head cleared, he decided that he had gone through enough. He retired from football to join the advertising firm of Young & Rubicam as a copy-writing trainee.

Kroll's first day on Madison Avenue was hardly spec-tacular. He showed up less than 24 hours after his final game and he was still groggy from the concussion. They sent him home. But, as he'd been doing all his life, he came back. Looking strangely out of place with the other trainees—most of them young girls just out of Smith and Vassar—he learned the business.

His first major success was a series of radio commercials for a beer company that featured hilarious conversations with a "2,500-year-old man." Kroll at first played one of the parts himself, but when the series was aired his voice was replaced by that of Dick Cavett. The commercial must have sold a lot of beer because from that point on, his rise at Y&R could be described only in understatement as "meteoric."

From trainee, he moved within a year into full status as a copy writer, then copy supervisor and creative supervisor. Within five years he was a vice-president, and in 1970 he moved into his present job, which also includes a position on the board of directors.

As a spokesman for his industry, Alex Kroll says, "We need more creativity today than ever before. We're the best salesmen when we're creating. In the final analysis, what counts is selling our clients' goods."

Talking about his own job, in which he has several hundred people working directly under him, Kroll acknowledges the significance of his efforts. "Nothing new will come out of the agency without my having thought about it, kicked it around and certified it," he comments simply.

Alex Kroll has made All-America in a business suit.

BILL COSBY
A SPORTING COMIC

WHEN BILL COSBY was growing up, home to him was a large and decaying tenement, filled with too many apartments, in North Philadelphia. He lived there with his mother and two brothers—his father was a cook in the Navy, and was away at sea most of the time—and, when not going to school or helping with the household chores, young Bill Cosby could usually be found in one place: the street.

The street, to most youngsters living in crowded cities like Philadelphia, was not only a roadway for cars. It was a playground and, although it had manhole covers instead of merry-go-rounds and pockmarked concrete instead of plush, rolling grass, it also had a particular beat of its own. The city streets are where some of the most unusual games in America are played.

When Bill Cosby was a youngster, a popular game was punchball. It was much like baseball, except that the players hit a rubber ball with their fists intead of a baseball with a bat. In young Cosby's neighborhood, (which also produced basketball stars Wilt Chamberlain, Walt Hazzard and Wally Jones), they didn't have bases, either; manhole covers were used

The "I Spy" star really can play tennis.

instead. A "punch" off a distant manhole cover straight away (second base) was the ultimate achievement. It was called a two-sewer hit. In baseball, it would have been a home run.

There was also stoopball, which required accuracy in bouncing a ball against the front steps of somebody's house. There was "Chinese handball," which required the player to hit the ball so it bounced once before it reached the wall, and there was stickball, of course, one of the most popular of the street games. Broomsticks and tin cans were used for bats and balls, and the game was quite like baseball, except that you don't slide as readily on concrete.

Bill was born on July 12, 1937, in Germantown Hospital, North Philadelphia, and by the time he was ten he'd grown to be an expert in all of the street games. By then, he also had his first set of heroes—Joe Louis and Sugar Ray Robinson, world-champion boxers; Buddy Young, a pro football star; Jackie Robinson, of the Brooklyn Dodgers, the first black man to play in the major leagues, and the Harlem Globetrotters' basketball team. When he wasn't playing in the streets, or working at odd jobs, he'd listen to radio broadcasts of his heroes' games in the family living room. Television was in its infancy then, and the Cosbys were among the many who didn't own a set.

But it wasn't all fun and games. At various times Bill shined shoes, worked as a handyboy in a grocery store and mixed drinks at the soda fountain in a drugstore.

Young Bill attended the Reynolds Elementary School and then the Mary Channing Wister School, where his fifth- and sixth-grade teacher was Mary Forchic. By now Bill had begun to develop a reputation as a clown with a high degree of intelligence but with little desire to do his homework. Miss Forchic wrote on one of Bill's report cards: "In this classroom there is one comedian and it is I. If you want to be one, grow up, get your own stage and get paid for it."

Nonetheless, Miss Forchic gave Bill an opportunity to perform—in class operettas. "I don't know how to act," he told the teacher, but he grinned when she retorted, "You've been acting from the first day in class."

It wasn't until he attended FitzSimons Junior High School that Bill actually became involved in organized sports.

Although he did not play on any of the school teams, he pitched for the Philadelphia Bombers' boys' team (formerly known as the Brown Bombers), and he also was a pitcher for the Police Athletic League team.

While at FitzSimons, he earned his way to Central High School, an all-male school for gifted young boys with IQ's of 120 or more. But he did not like it there and persuaded his mother to transfer him to Germantown High School, where he blossomed into an outstanding athlete. He was the leading ground-gainer on the Germantown football team and was the No. 1 high jumper on the track team. He also was elected by his teammates as captain of both squads.

But life was not easy for Bill at home, since he was the "man of the house" in his father's absence and had to assist his mother in looking after his two younger brothers.

"If your old man was home a lot, that meant he wasn't working steady," he explained. "If your old man had something steady, like my dad, it usually meant he had to be away from home so you didn't see him much. Either way, it was a hard thing for kids growing up."

Also, like many young, black males, Cosby had heard much about the world around him, but never got to see any of it since he rarely had the opportunity to leave the neighborhood streets or the Germantown High gym. Restless, and already nineteen years old, he decided to follow in his father's footsteps. He quit school and joined the Navy. He served as a physical therapist. During his four-year tour of duty he worked for his high school diploma and perfected his athletic skills. He had decided that when his hitch was up, he would go to college, get an education and become an athlete.

While in the Navy he competed extensively in the high jump and in one meet at the Quantico Marine Base in Virginia, he cleared six feet, five inches, a respectable height.

On leaving the service, he returned to Philadelphia and sought out Gavin White, then assistant director of athletics at Temple University. He told White that he wanted an athletic scholarship as a high jumper.

"What do you jump?" asked White.

"Seven feet," answered Cosby, with a smile.

"Well," said White, "that's too good for Temple. We only jump 5-8 around here."

They both laughed, and White, impressed with Cosby's desire, not to mention his good humor, awarded him a scholarship. So in September of 1960, at the age of twenty-three, when most students would already have graduated from college, Cosby entered Temple University as a freshman.

His recollections of his athletic career are still fresh in his mind. In keeping with the Cosby temperament, they are also humorous.

"Once we were competing in the National AAU meet," he said. "I had been high-jumping from eight in the morning to three in the afternoon, and I finally cleared 6-5. I got up from the pit, confident that I had won, only to find out that all the other jumpers, who had been standing around in their sweat suits watching me jump, were now going to start jumping at 6-5 and raise the bar from there. I finished 84th." (Actually, Cosby was 17th in that meet.)

"I used to love to psych out my opponents; con them into thinking that I was a lot better than I really was. Once, in the Middle-Atlantic meet, I was up against some of the best high jumpers in the East, including one guy who had whipped me earlier in the year by three or four inches. I decided something had to be done to even things out. So, while everybody was gathered around before the jumping started, I pointed to a slight lip of grass or dirt at the approach to the bar. Then I said, 'Fellows, don't come off that lip too hard because I saw a lot of guys slipping.'

"The other guys were impressed with the information and they started changing their steps whenever they approached the lip. Hell, even the guy who jumped 6-5 on me earlier wasn't able to jump six feet. I won the title easily—with a jump of six feet even." In addition, he finished fourth in the broad jump and was the second-leading scorer on the Temple team for the year with 50½ points.

Cosby also played football at Temple, where he was coached by Gavin White, who called him "the best blocker on the team." Cosby weighed 190 pounds for football (compared to 178 pounds in track), and was installed as a fullback, a

Bill Cosby: Football player at Temple University.

position he would later find unappealing. He wasn't much for the coaches' pep talks either.

"In my freshman season," he said, "we were invited to play in a special benefit game at night. It was freezing cold, there were few spectators in the stands to watch us, and the lights in the stadium were so bad people had to light matches to see. The coach decided that something had to be done to fire us up, and he decided to give us a pep talk. He said, 'We've got to go out there and show them that we're not city hicks and they can't do this to us!' So, he's in the locker room and we're all dressed in our uniforms and ready to go out onto the field and he's yelling at us. 'Let me hear you say, *"Kill!"* ' he screamed.

" '*Kill!*' we answered.

" 'Let me hear you say, *"Fight!"* ' he said.

" '*Fight!*' we said.

" 'Let me hear you say, *"We want to win!"* ' he demanded.

" '*We want to win!*' we shouted.

" 'Are you ready?'

" 'Yeah, we're ready.'

" 'Now go out there and get 'em . . .'

"All of us jumped up and started screaming our heads off and we started for the door. Then it got really embarrassing.

"The door was locked, and we couldn't get out."

When he made the varsity, under Coach George Makris, Cosby wasn't happy playing football any longer. He wanted to be a halfback and catch passes, but Makris installed him as a fullback (second-string) because he thought Cosby was a better blocker than a runner or a pass receiver. Cosby, blocking furiously, had his collarbone broken in three places.

Indeed, the experience of being a second-string blocking fullback did not sit too well with Cosby. He decided to get a job after practice to acquire some spending money, and he began thinking about other things, like making people laugh.

He took a job as a bartender in a nightclub called the Cellar, and started serving jokes with the drinks. Soon his comic routines behind the bar were so entertaining to the customers that he decided to go onto the stage of the club and see if he could still make them laugh. So responsive were his audiences that he decided to forget about a football career altogether and become a comic instead. He quit Temple after his second year.

He had almost made the Dean's List, an honor given only to top students.

As Bill started along the nightclub circuit, he dipped into his background in the Philadelphia streets and in Temple sports and he found that sports stories made his audiences laugh.

"Funny," he said, "but I used to think that what I went through in the streets was unique only to the kids in Philadelphia. But when I got out on the road, I found that kids in Akron and Cincinnati and Louisville and Los Angeles were doing the same things I did. White kids and black kids."

After two years on the road, Cosby broke one of the biggest color barriers in entertainment and became the "Jackie Robinson of television." In 1965, he was chosen to be the first black man to star in a major television series—"I Spy." In it, coincidentally, he even had a sports-oriented role; he was a secret agent who had, as his cover, the job of a tennis player. So successful was the show that not only did Cosby's own career take off like a rocket, but he opened the door to television for other black actors who had been kept outside for many years.

Bill won an Emmy Award—television's highest prize—for his performances as Alexander Scott, tennis pro and espionage agent, and a few years later, he wound up with his own show, titled simply, "The Bill Cosby Show." Again, he was in a sports-oriented role, that of Chet Kincaid, mild-mannered junior high school physical education teacher and coach. Also, there were special shows, guest appearances and the nightclub circuit—all with big fees.

By the time he turned thirty, Bill Cosby was a millionaire. He bought a home in Beverly Hills and moved into it with his wife Camille, and his two daughters. But even to this day, he has not forgotten about sports nor has he forgotten the youngsters who are still playing punchball and "Chinese handball" in the streets of our American cities.

With humorous stories about sports, Cosby has been able to reach his audiences. Once he has them in his grasp, he almost always drops in a story or two which, although funny, still get his point across—that black people in America still have problems and let's not forget it.

His routines about his playing days at Temple are par-

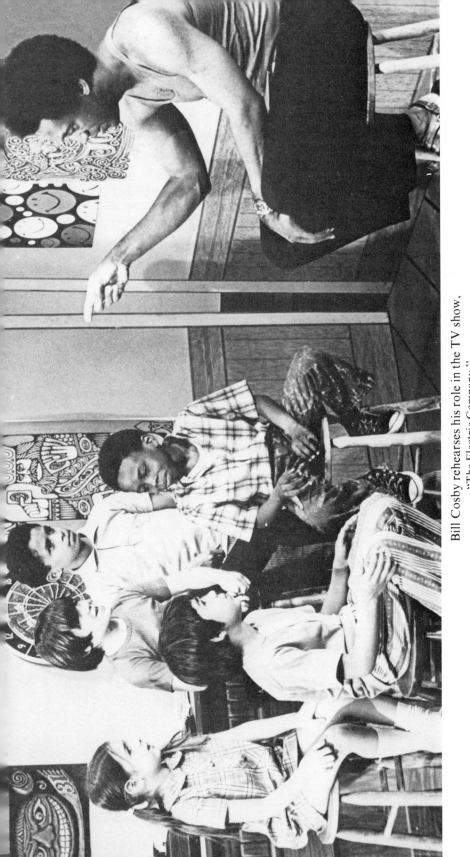

Bill Cosby rehearses his role in the TV show, "The Electric Company."

ticularly hilarious, although he obviously was a dedicated athlete and he took sports very seriously during the two years he was there. When asked about his athletic career at Temple, he will say: "Yeah, I was a second-string fullback; that means nothin'. But I was great on defense and I lasted out the season."

But to nightclub patrons, he may give the following routine:

"Now, when I was playing football at Temple, I was a defensive halfback and a chicken defensive halfback at that. My favorite excuse to the coach, after missing a tackle, was, 'I got faked out of position.' As a matter of fact, I used to go to great lengths, if a guy was running hard enough, to find somebody to block me out. Many times, I would spot a guy twenty-five yards away and fall down because I would figure he might throw a block at me.

"We used to play another game at Temple called 'Who Was That?' The coach would get the whole team together after a game and show movies of us playing. The coach would stop the film and say, 'All right, who was that?' Then you had to stand up and the coach would give it to you. Well, I was caught many times in 'Who Was That?' because I happened to be one of the few blacks on the team, so it was very easy to pick me out."

Cosby gave up his athletic scholarship at Temple to become a comic, and he has said that he has no regrets about the decision. Nor does he regret not having been able to play professional football. Emlen Tunnell, a scout for the New York Giants, had offered Bill a tryout. "It would have been a tough life for me, lying on my back in those stadiums every Sunday, looking up at the blue sky . . . with cleat marks running up and down my chest," Cosby says.

But Cosby's routines have disguised a deeper message. In a subtle way he is fighting for the rights of black people through his stories. He was a pioneer in his profession, and his sports humor has been the cornerstone of his success.

He has helped others succeed in another way too. In the "I Spy" series, which ran on television screens for several years, more and more black actors began appearing in roles as a result of Cosby's success. In "The Bill Cosby Show" young blacks were cast in many roles, too. In between, Cosby went out of his way to help get starring roles for black actors in other shows.

In recent years, Cosby has been speaking at college campuses; hosting children's shows and working as a commentator for TV shows on black history. He is in great demand as a master of ceremonies and has given out Emmy Awards to television's greatest stars as well as awards to athletes at high school banquets.

He also occasionally plays with the Harlem Globetrotters, basketball's most famous team. Although he is not as flashy a ball-handler as the rest of the Globetrotters, he handles the ball quite well and is a fine shooter. "It's something I've always dreamed of," Cosby said. "When I play with the Globetrotters, I can be funny and play some good basketball at the same time. For me, I guess that's the perfect combination."

Although he may not be famous for his play with the Globetrotters or for his football prowess at Temple University, Bill Cosby will be remembered for something considerably more important: the breakthrough he made for himself and for other black people, in the television industry.

Punchball on the streets of Philadelphia hasn't changed, but television, thanks to the impact of Bill Cosby, will never be the same.

BENJAMIN SPOCK
HE ROWED HIS OWN WAY

YOUNG BEN SPOCK was afraid of the dinosaur that lived at the bottom of Mansfield Horner's cellar stairs. Mansfield Horner was Ben's friend. Mansfield told him about the dinosaur and Ben believed it.

Ben was also afraid of lions that he imagined lived and lurked in a tall grassy area near his house on Cold Spring Street in New Haven, Connecticut.

Ben Spock grew up with many of the fears and vague terrors that plague most young children. He also grew up with many of the same wistful longings and joys and dreams and curiosities that are shared, or have been shared, by us all.

As a child, he gave no hint of what he would become. He seemed to follow the norm for his time and his place. He was born on May 2, 1903, the first of Mildred and Benjamin Spock's six children. His "place" was in a well-to-do family (his father was a railroad executive) living in a conventional, cheery frame house with a porch and four cherry trees in the backyard. Summers were spent in desolate coastal towns in Maine.

His mother was a strict, if not in fact, a fierce disciplinarian.

Dr. Spock was in the forefront of the struggle for peace.

For example, because she wanted her children to be rugged, she often made them sleep, whether winter or summer, in an unheated canvas tent that she put up on the roof of the front porch.

For punishment, Mrs. Spock would sometimes lock her children in a closet for an entire day. Perhaps it was no wonder that Ben Spock did not begin to speak until he was almost three, and then he spoke with painful slowness.

He was too frightened to be defiant. And when he did something that was "unconventional," it seemed he did it not because he was a rebel but because he was a victim.

When he was eleven years old, he suffered a humiliating experience. He was out sailing one summer day with a friend named Bill, Ben's governess, Miss Ogden, and Miss Ogden's friend. This was 1914, a time of parasols and high-button shoes and long flowing dresses, and it seems that Miss Ogden's friend had lifted her dress above her ankles. In those days, shocking! Ben stared at this uncommon sight. Miss Ogden saw the young boy "ogling" her friend's well-turned ankles and gave him a sharp reprimand.

Ben was so humbled, he spent the rest of the afternoon with eyes downcast and his guilty conscience was filled with the knowledge that he was some kind of sex fiend.

Obviously, though, Ben Spock was growing up. At age fifteen he was six feet four inches tall and weighed 100 pounds. He was so long and thin that someone commented that if he drank strawberry soda it would register in him like a thermometer.

He was what is known as a "preppie," having gone to Hamden Hall Country Day School in Hamden, Connecticut, and Phillips Academy in Andover, Massachusetts.

At Andover, he began to develop a sense of himself. Much of that, a growing feeling of confidence through achievement, came from athletics. Andover, one of the finest and oldest preparatory schools in the United States, encouraged the old Greek tradition of nimble mind and sound body. Not only did Ben Spock make the honor society for his academic work at Andover, but he was also a decent enough player to make the club soccer team and to compete as a high jumper in track and field.

His long, thin legs helped propel him over the high-jump bar and into a new world: the world of the athlete. He fancied himself as such after winning third place in a track meet and eventually earning a school letter.

Here, his reasoning and his ways were accepted, not considered different. He had been embarrassed about his slow way of speaking, about his gaunt height, and he had been made self-conscious by the rigid child-rearing methods of his mother. His parents had also dressed him oddly, making him wear old-fashioned wool suits in summer.

Athletics was a springboard for him. As a high jumper, Ben Spock seemed to be leaping out of his confining childhood into a more free-swinging young manhood.

Ben went to Yale, where his father had gone before him. He was little concerned with academics. Politics hardly existed for him. Two things did interest him: girls, called "flappers" in those days, and personal achievement.

In the early 1920s, personal achievement or "success" was measured at Yale in sports and in extracurricular activities. There were societies, clubs and organizations one had to belong to if one was to "make it" at Yale.

There was also athletics. It seemed that almost every kind of social activity, such as dances, parties and so forth, revolved around a sporting activity. And how much easier it was for a young man, if he were an athletic hero, to get into campus organizations like Skull and Bones, Scroll and Key or the Elihu Club.

When Ben Spock was a Yale freshman, in 1921, the most important sports on campus were crew, football, hockey and swimming. Ben thought of himself as a high jumper. He had jumped 5 feet, 6 inches at Andover and that mark was good enough to place him on the Yale freshman track team. He also hoped that his expected excellence in the sport would provide him with the social recognition he so desired. But as it turned out, he was not long for the sport of high jumping, which was just as well, since 5-6 turned out to be his absolute ceiling. He never again jumped higher.

One day in his freshman year he was on his way to high-jump practice when he stopped to watch the varsity crew practice on the rowing machines in the gymnasium.

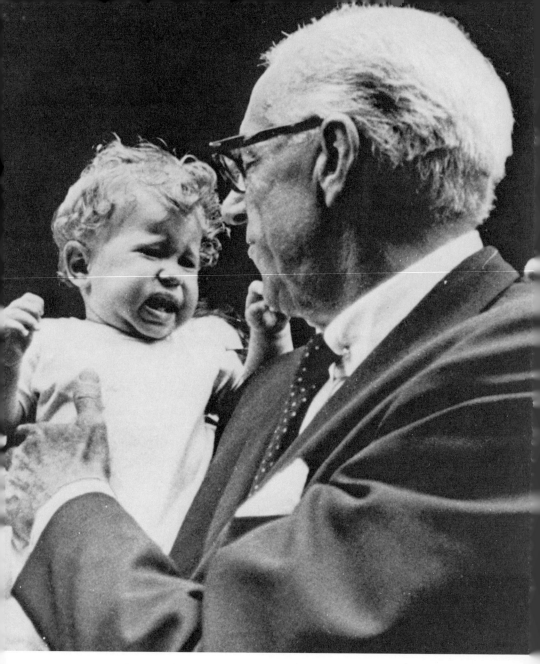

Dr. Spock was known as "the modern father of our country."

"A chinless, gawky wonder," as he would later describe himself, freshman Spock stood quietly and listened to the crank and grunt of the oarsmen.

"What sport do you go out for?" demanded a booming voice. It belonged to Langhorn Gibson, a tall, handsome, intimidating person who happened to be standing alongside Ben. Gibson was crew captain.

"High jumping," said Ben softly. He wanted to say, "High jumping, *sir*," but managed to swallow that last word.

"Why don't you go out for a *man's* sport?" It was not a question but a challenge.

Ben Spock was not insulted. He was thrilled. After all, he was not only being noticed by this distinguished upperclassman, he was in fact being *spoken* to by him. Ben rushed right off and signed up for the crew, though he had never been in a shell before.

Over one hundred boys went out for the various crew teams that year, and each of them made one of the teams. The boys were assigned to eight-man crews lettered in order of ability.

"I landed on the M freshman crew," Ben Spock proudly told friends. "A, B, C, D, E, F, G, H, I, J, K, L, M—that one."

Ben was determined to be a success in this, the proudest of Yale sports. His height, as luck would have it, proved an advantage. His long legs could give a push to the rowing motion that hastened the power and speed of the blade stroke.

He worked hard in practice. In his sophomore year, he moved up from sophomore *F* to junior varsity. And though the crew lost two of its three races, the season of 1923 was still deemed a success: Yale had beaten its arch-rival, Harvard.

In his junior year, Ben made the varsity. A stupendous achievement. And it was a stupendous crew. It was good enough to win several major races and then to be named the United States representative in the Olympic Games in Paris in 1924.

Ben Spock, seventh oar, was good enough to be called by the *Boston Post,* "the best individual performer." The *Post* article continued: "In all the races which were rowed by Yale in 1924, (Spock) passed the stroke down his side of the shell with such smoothness and accuracy that he kept all forward of him in line, and between him and the stroke there was a touch of imperceptible sympathy that had as much to do with rendering Yale crews perfect as any other cause cultivated by Coach Ed Leader."

The team left for Paris on June 21 aboard the S.S. *Homeric*. A brass band and a crowd of shouting, straw-hat-waving students saw them off. On the way over, under the stern eye of Coach Leader, the team did daily calisthenics and worked out on the rowing machines that the coach had placed on deck.

The trip had one high point for Ben Spock, and one low point. The high point came at a dance on the boat. Gloria Swanson, then a stunning young Hollywood movie star, was on the boat. On the last night of the seven-day voyage, she succumbed to various Yale schemes to get her to dance with the crew members.

She danced with each one, and when it was Ben's turn he was introduced by fellow crewman Archie Quarrier. "Here's Big Ben," Archie said.

"Big Ben, but no alarm," the elegant Miss Swanson said.

Ben was almost floored by the witticism, but he managed to remain on his long legs for the dance.

The low point? That had come the day before, at another dance. Ben was dancing with a young lady. No one else was interested in cutting in on her. Spock, too shy and too kind to leave her alone, kept dancing past curfew. All his teammates had departed. Then Coach Leader strode onto the floor and hollered: "Spock! Get to your cabin." Spock was off in a flash.

Again, as in earlier days, when Ben Spock did something "off limits," he did it not as a rebel but as a victim.

In Paris, Coach Leader found the official huts in the Olympic Village unacceptable for his team. So for the seventeen days prior to the race, the Yale team managers, with money provided by interested alumni, were able to rent a large house in a choice suburb of Saint Germain-en-Laye. And the team members ate their meals at a gourmet restaurant next door.

The crew practiced twice a day on the river Seine. They were, of course, well fed, well rested (Coach Leader insisted on afternoon naps and 9:30 curfews) and were undisputed favorites, being taller, younger and heavier than all competitors. ("Heavier" may have been disputed by some, since the 1925 Yale yearbook described the Spanish team as a "beefy boatload from Madrid.")

The Americans won the 2,000-meter trial heat in record-breaking time, 5:51. The final heat was held at 6:30 P.M. on July 17. It was to be the United States against Great Britain, Canada and Italy.

The evening was warm, there was little breeze. Ben Spock's large, strong hands were moist as they grasped the oars.

There was a sizable Yale group in the grandstands. They were silent now. There was no gun to start the race. A Frenchman shouted, *"Partez!"*—"Go!" As soon as he pronounced the "P," the Yale team was off and rowing furiously.

In just 20 strokes, or 30 seconds, it had a 15-foot lead. Ben Spock was working those blades in the water as he had never done before.

The Yale crew increased its lead to 75 feet at the halfway mark. The race seemed over almost before it had begun. The Americans came in nearly 300 feet ahead of second-place Canada.

Ben Spock, upon receiving the gold medal, was so choked with pride he could barely breathe.

He had become a success beyond his fondest dreams. As an Olympic star, he was, of course, invited to join virtually any campus society he desired.

He met and soon married a lovely, graceful young lady named Jane Cheney. After Yale, he went to medical school and eventually became a pediatrician. But not just a run-of-the-crib baby doctor. *The* baby doctor. In fact, in years to come, he would be called, only half-jokingly, the post-World War II father of our country.

Dr. Benjamin Spock wrote a book, published in 1946, which revolutionized baby care. The book is called *The Common Sense Book of Baby and Child Care.* It has sold over twenty-five million copies, third only to the Bible and Shakespeare. It has been printed in dozens of languages. It is estimated that one out of every four American babies has been brought up on the book.

The book changed the general concept of child-rearing.

Ben Spock, third from left, rowed for Yale's Olympic Crew.

"Where I came in," Dr. Spock explained, "was in pop-
ularizing progressive education and Freudianism." Progressive education has emphasized "doing and feeling" what is
right as opposed to superstition. Freud insisted that a child
doesn't have to be intimidated to be responsive; he valued the
power of love over fear.

This so-called "permissive" child-care attitude has resulted
in thick criticism in some quarters. In fact, in the 1960s, Vice
President Agnew blamed student activists on Spock's book.
"The students were raised on a book by Dr. Spock, and a
paralyzing permissive philosophy pervades every policy they
espouse," the Vice President said.

Dr. Spock, though, never considers himself a "per-
missivist." In the end, his child-rearing philosophy is summed
up in the advice to parents in the first two sentences of the
book: "Trust yourself. You know more than you think you
do."

Dr. Spock, now a tall, white-haired, distinguished physi-
cian, probably would not have been nearly as controversial if
he had not entered the political arena late in life, in the 1960s.

"I didn't become a rebel, really, until I was in my 60s," he
says.

He had been a conservative Republican most of his life, but
gradually began to espouse Democratic, and then radical,
platforms. The arms race, the cold war, the Vietnam War, the
racial conflicts at home, the disastrous economic problems in
America, the generation gap, all this shook his philosophical
foundations.

"What was the use, I said to myself, of bringing up healthy,
well-adjusted children if they were going to die in a senseless
war, or even be frustrated in their adult lives in a maladjusted,
malfunctioning country?"

Soon he was marching in protests. In 1968, he was arrested
and indicted for helping and conspiring with draft evaders. He
was found guilty, along with a handful of others. But a court of
appeals overturned the convictions; Dr. Spock was found only
to have "urged" young men to burn draft cards—not to have
"conspired" with them to do it.

In 1971, he became the stand-in candidate for President on
the People's Party. The People's Party is a loose alliance of

various peace movement groups. Dr. Spock, when he accepted the candidacy, knew there was no realistic chance for him actually to become President of the United States. This didn't bother him. His candidacy was part of his outraged, moralistic statement against the ugliness of the times, and a hopeful reach for something better.

How strange, looking back, to see so much drama and worldwide revolutionary thought set in motion by someone who was, in his own words, "a shy kid who needed constant reassurance."

The transition from a retiring child to a strongly independent man came about in those Yale crew days, Dr. Spock says today.

In his golden years he proudly remembers how he helped row Yale to victory in 1924 in Paris. He demonstrates the stroke, his lined face grimacing, teeth clenched, eyes narrowed behind glasses. He grunts and pushes his imaginary oars back and forth. When he finishes, he lets out a hearty laugh. "It's the only sport played sitting down and going backwards," he says.

"But I beam visibly when I think about being on that crew team. It was my greatest triumph. I've never quite outgrown it. Being a successful athlete was one of the most important things to ever happen to me. It was only then that I dared question whether to be like anyone else. It gave me confidence. Don't be afraid to be different, be *proud* to be different."

WHIZZER
WHITE
ALL-AMERICAN ON THE BENCH

THE MARBLE COLUMNS and the heavy mahogany furniture, so dominant when the stately courtroom is empty, seem dwarfed by the presence of the nine black-robed men sitting behind the massive bench. The Supreme Court of the United States has been called to order, and the crowded room is respectfully hushed.

Vital decrees are issued from this imposing building across the street from the U.S. Capitol in Washington, D.C. The Chief Justice, Warren Burger, turns to Associate Justice Byron White and asks for an opinion.

Justice White, who has been rocking slowly in his leather chair during the early moments of the session, delivers an opinion in slow, matter-of-fact tones.

When he has concluded his remarks, Justice White leans back in his chair, smiling faintly. He is relaxed, confident. An observer notices his trim 6-foot-2-inch frame, assured posture and clear voice. He is clearly a man in command of his own destiny.

Whizzer!

That's what they called Associate Justice Byron White when

When sworn in, White, 44, was the youngest in the Supreme Court.

he was an All-American tailback at the University of Colorado in 1937, an outstanding back with the Pittsburgh Pirates (later to become the Steelers) in 1938, and with the Detroit Lions in 1940 and 1941. Byron White had been in control of his own destiny long before he donned the black robe of a U.S. Supreme Court Justice.

On a cold November afternoon in 1937, in Salt Lake City, Utah, the University of Utah football team set out to do what every one of Colorado's opponents for two years had attempted: Stop Whizzer White! For two quarters Utah had succeeded, holding White and the Buffaloes to a 0-0 tie as 18,000 Homecoming spectators roared approval.

In the third quarter, Byron White began delivering decisions. He kicked a 15-yard field goal. Then, after Utah had taken a 7-3 lead, White picked up a bouncing punt on his own five-yard line, and began stiff-arming and zigzagging his way up the field 95 yards for a touchdown. Later, as tailback of the team, he called his own signal, "28-right," a play off the single wing in which White took the snap from center, circled wide to his right, then sped 57 yards for another touchdown and a 17-7 Colorado victory.

His 1937 output of 16 touchdowns, 23 extra points and one field goal topped the country in scoring and led Colorado to an undefeated season. Then he changed clothes, to a basketball uniform, and helped Colorado gain the finals of the National Invitational Tournament in New York City. In between all the games and practice sessions, he found the time to win a Rhodes Scholarship to Oxford University, Oxford, England.

To Byron White, sports were something to enjoy, the way a fellow delights in a game of neighborhood softball or a day of fishing on a quiet stream. He could never realistically accept the acclaim thrust upon him for his accomplishments on a football field or basketball court. Yet he was a gracious idol, even when it came to tolerating the unjudicial nickname of Whizzer.

"I didn't mind the name Whizzer when I was a football player," he said. "It was a compliment, and still is, although I'm afraid I left the nickname behind long ago."

Today, Byron White, an Associate Justice since April 16,

1962, limits his whizzing to frequent workouts in the Supreme Court Building's gymnasium and a round of golf when his schedule permits. He has been seen at RFK Stadium watching the Washington Redskins, and he sometimes attends games of the Detroit Lions and Pittsburgh Steelers. His favorite weekend activity, however, is relaxing in his McLean, Virginia, home with his wife Marion and their two teenage children, Nancy and Barney.

A life of sport is something very distant and foreign to the Justice, and his reluctance to become actively involved again is evidenced by his personally directed efforts to stay off the sports pages. He was once considered a candidate for the job of Baseball Commissioner, and was often sought after to appear at sports banquets. Justice White said no to baseball—and to most banquet program chairmen. He wasn't interested.

Justice White's day in the sports limelight ended in 1941. He's been trying to tell people that ever since.

"The fundamental reason for playing competitive sports is to get some experience," he said. "Sports constantly make demands on the participant for top performance, and they develop integrity, self-reliance and initiative. They teach you a lot about working in groups without being unduly submerged in the group.

"Probably the best reason for taking part in contact sports is that you like them," Justice White continued. "Some people who are insecure, however, have built themselves into pretty admirable people through the confidence they've gained from competing in contact sports. It has given them the shot in the arm they needed, and they've carried it on into other activities."

Justice White's "shot in the arm" was his own initiative, which surfaced even before he reached high school age. He was born June 8, 1917, in Ft. Collins, Colorado. He grew up in Wellington, a town of 350 people. His father was manager of a lumber supply company. By the time Byron was seven, he was adding to the family income by planting and harvesting beets with his brother Sam, four years his elder. The White brothers earned between a dollar and two dollars a day, depending on how much work they did, and they saved their money for clothes and other necessities. High school for Byron White consisted of harvesting beets, playing sports and studying. Byron's father, Alpha Albert White, was intent on his two sons going to college.

"I would rather see you win one medal for scholarship than forty ball games," Alpha Albert White told his younger son.

Byron was an A-student throughout high school, and he won the one scholarship the University of Colorado awarded each year to the No. 1 student in each of the state's towns. His brother had won the scholarship four years earlier.

Byron was an all-around athlete in Wellington, participating in football, basketball, baseball and track. Although he missed one season of football because of a broken shoulder, his potential was much in evidence when he left Wellington for the University of Colorado in the fall of 1934.

In his freshman year, he studied chemistry, mathematics and science, but by the end of his sophomore year, he had switched to humanities and economics, with a career in law already entrenched in his mind.

"My parents wanted me to be what I wanted to be," White said. "They had a pretty simple prescription for living. You worked hard, did as well as you could and were considerate of other people's feelings."

On the football field, he had a satisfactory freshman campaign, accomplishing enough good things to attract the attention of the varsity coaches. In his sophomore year, he was a third-string tailback, making his long-awaited varsity debut in the opening game against Oklahoma. He immediately twisted his knee.

"I had a hard time with my knee in my sophomore year," White said. "It was swelling up like a balloon, and I could only play parts of two games. I decided I wouldn't let them operate. If I couldn't play athletics, then what the hell. Every day the knee was taped. When you have a bum knee like that you develop a protective reaction. Anytime anyone got within a hundred yards of me, I'd make damn sure my knee was bent. You can't get hurt as long as it's bent."

The knee withstood a season of basketball, and when Byron showed up for the start of football practice in 1936 he was reasonably confident it would hold up.

He became the starting tailback, which meant he did all Colorado's passing, punting and much of the running. His tremendously long and accurate punts remain legendary statistics at Colorado, as do his breath-taking punt returns.

White's knee problem actually aided his punting. "My knee was all right, except when I kicked the ball at normal height," he said. "So I learned to kick low. It was great for accuracy and kicking into the wind but not much good for getting down under punts."

Colorado's most explosive weapon was the Whizzer White punt return. Coach Bunnie Oakes had a theory that punt returners would gain more yardage by catching kicks in full stride, rather than waiting in one spot for the ball to drop from the sky. White handled this difficult assignment brilliantly, scoring numerous touchdowns on runbacks and taking the Buffs into excellent field position with others. He also managed to survive the seemingly suicidal maneuver, probably because he practiced the play one hour each day.

Performing as tailback in Oakes' single wing formation, White became a terror throughout the Rocky Mountain Conference, slashing off tackle and outrunning people at the flanks. In the open field, it was considered nearly impossible for a single defender to bring him down. He used the stiff-arm as a lance, cutting down foes as fast as they arose.

His coach said of White: "He was a great triple threat, fast, shifty in the open with his 190 pounds. A fine passer capable of throwing accurately at any length, and an excellent long-distance punter who could place his kicks. He also was a good kickoff man and a very accurate place-kicker. His signal-calling was almost perfect."

At this point in his career, the accolades began to mount up as White's fame spread across the country. "I had a little difficulty adjusting to all the publicity," he said. "I thought it was exaggerated, and besides it set me off from other people. As much as anything else, you never felt you were alone any place. You couldn't go anywhere without somebody wanting to come up and talk to you. But I figured the newspaper people knew what they were doing and it was their job to do it, so I went along with it as best I could."

By the conclusion of his junior year, White not only had the reputation of being a fine football, basketball and baseball player, he had already won his Phi Beta Kappa key in scholastic achievement. In his senior year, Colorado churned through the regular season unbeaten and untied and became the first Rocky Mountain area team to be invited to a Bowl game. Despite White's interception of a pass and run for a touchdown, and pass for another, all in the first ten minutes of the game, Colorado lost to Rice, 28-14, in the Cotton Bowl.

Between practices for his final college football game, White went to San Francisco to compete for a Rhodes Scholarship, worth $4,000, for two years of study at Oxford. He won the scholarship.

In four years at Colorado, he had played three varsity sports, had been named to the All-America football team, and had reached the top academically with straight A's, with the exception of B's in public speaking and sociology.

White did not intend to play professional football, particularly after having been selected for the Rhodes Scholarship. He wavered, however, when, in 1938, Art Rooney, owner of the Pittsburgh team, offered him a $15,000 contract, an astronomical amount for a pro football player at that time. Byron would have rejected Rooney's offer, except for the fact that his brother Sam, also a Rhodes Scholar, had arranged with Oxford officials for his younger brother to start in January—after the football season.

So Whizzer White became a professional football player for Pittsburgh in the National Football League. He justified his salary by becoming the first rookie in history to win the National Football League's rushing championship, gaining 567 yards. Then he went to Oxford.

"I liked pro ball better than the college game," he said. "In the professional league there is no such thing as a soft game. The money part of it isn't nearly as important as some people make out. Once the whistle blows you play for the same reason you always play games. You play to win."

Byron White reveled in the academic atmosphere of Oxford. He toured France and Germany, living for two months in Munich during the summer of 1939. It was there that he spent several evenings in the company of a young man named John F. Kennedy, whose father was United States Ambassador to England.

When the war in Europe started, White went home and

President John F. Kennedy meets with his friend, Whizzer White.

enrolled at Yale Law School. He did not play football in 1939, but after the Detroit Lions purchased his contract he agreed to work for them in 1940. Again, he led the NFL in rushing. The next season with the Lions, a mediocre team, was White's last in pro ball. He joined the Navy a few days after the Japanese attacked Pearl Harbor. He gained seven battle stars and two bronze stars as an intelligence officer in the Pacific theatre and reached the rank of full lieutenant.

His friendship with Jack Kennedy continued and intensified when White was one of the intelligence officers assigned to write a report on the sinking of Kennedy's PT boat.

After the war, White returned to Yale, receiving his LL.B. degree, *magna cum laude,* in November of 1946. He then went to work as a law clerk for Justice Fred M. Vinson, of the U.S. Supreme Court, serving until 1947. After that he returned to Colorado to work for a small law firm in Denver.

He became involved in politics, starting as a precinct committeeman, later a ward captain and then as manager for various candidates.

"When people turn up their noses at politics it's a great mistake," he has said. "It merely serves to perpetuate the very thing people criticize in politics—that it's a dirty business. Everyone in this country has an obligation to take part in politics. That's the foundation, the most important principle on which our system is built. If our system is to work, people must intelligently elect their representatives in the legislatures and the Congress and their local government. And the best way to do that is to get their feet wet in politics."

White was content in his law practice and with life in Denver when, in 1960, he was selected to head up a Colorado Committee for John F. Kennedy, presidential hopeful, prior to the Democratic Convention. He was asked to lead a National Citizens Committee for Kennedy, which he did. When Kennedy became President, White accepted the appointment of Deputy Attorney General, serving admirably in that position until April of 1962, when the President appointed him to the Supreme Court.

On the Supreme Court, he has been a vigorous supporter of civil rights enforcement and a conservative in matters of civil liberties. He is known among observers of the court for his probing questions.

Whizzer White runs for All-Stars against Washington Redskins.

Retaining his easygoing manner, White is considered one of the most approachable of the Justices, on an informal basis. He evidently still believes the sports aspect of his life has been overplayed, evidenced by the fact that since joining the Supreme Court he has remained aloof from Washington's sports-writing fraternity, whose members have often sought him out for features and other stories.

He has stayed in the sports spotlight, however, by virtue of organizations such as the National Football League Players Association, which presents an annual award to the member possessing "the qualities" of Justice White—"scholar, athlete, patriot, humanitarian and public servant."

Past winners of this award include Bart Starr, of the Green Bay Packers, Willie Davis, of the Green Bay Packers, Ed Meador, of the Los Angeles Rams, Gale Sayers, of the Chicago Bears and Kermit Alexander, of the San Francisco 49ers.

"The award has been established by the professional football players of America to acknowledge our debt of gratitude to one of our own," reads the inscription on the trophy.

The U.S. Supreme Court has benefited from Justice White's service, and so has the country.

ABOUT THE EDITORS

PHYLLIS HOLLANDER is a graduate of the University of Michigan and an avid outdoorswoman. She is senior editor of Associated Features, Inc., packagers of sports books. Her writing credits include chapters in *Strange But True Football Stories* and *They Dared to Lead*, which she co-edited with her sportswriter husband, Zander Hollander. She also wrote *American Women in Sports*.

ZANDER HOLLANDER is a veteran author and editor. For twenty years he covered a variety of sports for the New York *World-Telegram*, and he is currently the president of Associated Features. Mr. Hollander wrote *Yankee Batboy*; co-authored *The Home-Run Story*; edited *Great American Athletes of the 20th Century, Baseball Lingo,* and *The Modern Encyclopedia of Basketball*; and co-edited *The Complete Encyclopedia of Ice Hockey*.
   Phyllis and Zander Hollander live with their son and daughter in Baldwin, New York.